HOW TO BE A F*CKING LADY

A Modern Guide to Being Charming & Fierce AF

D1604147

Miss J

ISBN: 978-0-578-72258-0

Table of Contents

Dedication

This book is dedicated to my grandmother Leida
and the fierce women she raised.

EXCLUSIVE GIFT FOR MY STYLISH READERS

This book is just the beginning…

I believe every woman deserves to create her own makeover story.
She deserves to show up Stylish & Confident.
Why? Because confident women build legacies.

On that stylish note…

I'm GIFTING YOU my mini-Style Course here:

www.JudithGaton.com/stylecourse

~MISS J

About the Author

Miss J is a stylist, certified life coach, and lawyer. She is your professor of glam and elegance. Through her signature course Style Masterclass, she teaches her clients that thought work is the key to a lasting makeover. Through confidence coaching and mindset work, she helps her clients to see that they can dress and love the body they are in right now. When Style & Confidence are dialed in, women can go do the work they were created to do in the world. Her ultimate style philosophy: Confident Women Build Legacies.

To learn more about her work and to take a Free Personal Style Class go to www.judithgaton.com/stylecourse

Introduction

Welcome to *How to be a F*cking Lady, A Modern Guide to Being Charming & Fierce AF*. First, I must tell you this is not your grandmama's charm school. In this guide, you will learn about charm, etiquette, and how to show up like a lady boss. This guide is for the woman who has both brains and beauty and wants to show up accordingly.

This guide book is meant to celebrate vintage style and principles. It is of chief import that you know I adopt the vintage style, but not vintage values. I am not a proponent of adopting a set of behaviors that are antithetical to femininity or femaleness. Nor am I a proponent of misogyny and racism of bygone eras. Instead, I am proposing you take the concepts from the best charm schools in the 1940s and 1950s, and make them accessible, intelligible, and modern.

Much of the charm school curriculum from your grandmama's day still has relevance, but much from that time period was laced with cringey values that we can leave behind. I am re-writing and redefining the old charm school curriculum because a woman's desire to learn to speak, walk, stand, and converse is no longer solely to please, attract, or keep men.

I grew up in a predominantly female family. My grandmother had five daughters, I have four sisters, and my sister has three daughters. My cousins have mostly girl children. The lady leadership continues. This overwhelmingly female influence taught me a great deal about what it means to be female, feminine, and fierce. True to any family unit, we created our own charm school and etiquette to dictate how ladies behave. I have one aunt who puts it best when discussing these types of things, "It's because I'm such a freaking lady." She then dispenses the most practical advice.

One example of this is my grandmother, aunts, and mother always advise us to "pontes chu-ching," which is Nuyorican slang that loosely translates to "Get prettied up before you leave the house. Don't go out looking crazy."

My grandmother used to tell my mother and my aunt's, "Don't do good things that look bad." In other words, "Don't be seen as overly flirtatious, sit on a man's lap, or reach into his pocket." (Yeah, I will let you further interpret that one.) My mother also told my sisters and me, should we get into a fistfight, "You better come home looking worse than the other girl." My family etiquette, a code of social behavior, is definitely female, feminine, and *fierce.* As my aunts say, "It's because I'm such a freaking lady."

My family was and is still governed by these rules of etiquette. It was not until I experienced other etiquette codes in different settings that I realized the rest of my adult life would be a series of code-switching between being female and feminine, and learning when to throw in the fierce.

I realized that no matter how many etiquette books I read, I would continue to be confronted with the same thing. I was trying to learn how to become charming and learn etiquette from a group of writers that lived in a time and place that was most certainly "a man's world." The advice given was mainly about modifying your behavior so you could attract a man and keep him. Most of the advice regarding female relationships suggested you should appear empathetic and likable to your female friends. To be an asset to your husband seemed to be of chief import. It was a lot of the do's and don'ts without a real sense of **why?**

True to my own irreverent nature, I decided to write a book about how to be a freaking lady in a way that takes the best of past advice and modernizes it in a way that makes sense. There is value in "pontes chu-ching," or learning to dress like a lady. There is sound advice in being wary of your surroundings and the men around you. There is also value in deciding to show up fierce no matter how formidable your foe may appear.

I decided there needed to be a book for this female future. Learning to be a freaking lady is essential because women are increasingly up-wardly mobile, yet their given etiquette may not withstand a world that still operates as though it is a man's world. Being a freaking lady allows you to code-switch between the terms and familial concepts you were raised with while reconceptualizing them in a way that makes sense, is practical, and applicable.

For example, words like elegance, poise, gumption, and elocution have no meaning in our present day and age. You can understand their definitions, but fail to see their continued significance and relevance. What comes to mind is a line of skinny ladies parading around with a stack of books on their heads. So, let's spin and code-switch. Let's put some juice on old concepts and give them relevance.

Contrast that with words like chu-ching or phrases like "don't do good things that look bad," and you have a hell of a hot mess of mixed messages. Being a freaking lady is about how to sit, stand, and talk while being firm in your convictions and confidence.

In this guide, you will learn a modernized version of charm school subjects. I want you to love the vintage style, but not the values. Here, *Elegance* is all about becoming *stylish AF*. *Beauty* includes all women of every size and shape. *Elocution* is about how to talk and knowing when to shut your face. *Poise* is learning to rise up. *Gumption* is for the woman who has more than just a pretty face. *Pluck* is because you want to show up like a boss.

A freaking lady is female, feminine, and fierce. She models it for the women around her. Her way of being is a whole mood and a way of life. It is more than the reputation that precedes her. **WHY do we care? Because confident women leave legacies.**

ELEGANCE: How to be *Stylish AF*

Issamood

Elegance is twofold – appearance and manner. How you dress and how you act. To be elegant is to dress and be stylish. It is both what you put on your body and how you behave. Elegance is a mindset that becomes a mood and, eventually, a way of life. It is like adding *AF* to the end of an adjective. Pretty is ok, but *Pretty AF* is a mood. You can be fancy, but *Fancy AF* is a whole level mood. To be elegant is to be a woman who is *Stylish AF*—issamood.

Growing up, my favorite movie was *Gigi*. It is a musical set in Paris in the early 1900s. The story is about a young girl whose Aunt Alicia gives her lessons every week on how to be a lady. Her Auntie is a beautiful older woman who teaches her how to dress, eat, sit, and stand. In one scene, Aunt Alicia teaches Gigi how to pick out jewels and gemstones – and even spot a fake. (The practical stuff you need to know in case your lover tries to buy you a knock-off pearl necklace.)

There is a fashion show moment where Gigi is trying on gown after gown, and each one Gigi likes, her aunt rejects. Each one her aunt loves, Gigi hates. It is the ultimate makeover movie in technicolor 1950s musical amazingness. When I was younger, I wished I had an Aunt Alicia who was rich and would teach me how to be fancy. The critics loved this movie. It won eight Oscars in 1956, even Best Picture. However, like all things romanticized in the past, this movie isn't without the usual pretty lipstick on a pig.

Now, when I watch this movie as an adult, there is some pretty cringey craziness that I never picked up on before. The Auntie is kind of a hoe (no judgment), and she is training Gigi also to be a high-paid hoe. Gigi's mama abandoned her, so she had to live with her grand-mama, who is broke. The goal is not even to get Gigi married to an old wealthy dude. Nope, just some dude who is willing to "compensate her well" for being his "companion" until he is onto the next one. Yup, lovely little technicolor dream.

This is very similar to much of the old advice on beauty, charm, and elegance. It is pretty much lipstick on a pig. Not always, but enough of the time that we must examine it and take the lipstick and leave the pig. To be elegant is to be pleasingly graceful in appearance and manner. If we look at only past definitions of elegance, we would be relegated to white table cloths, fine dining, and a certain style of dress that is appealing only to men or mean old ladies. Like I said, let's keep the lipstick and leave the pig.

How Do We Become *Stylish AF*?

How do we become *Stylish AF* without a rich Auntie to guide us? No rich auntie needed. You have Miss J, your professor of glam and elegance, to walk you through your makeover story. I didn't have an Aunt Alicia, nor was I born into privilege. But I never thought, "Oh, well. I can't be stylish." Instead, I take the lipstick and leave the pig. From *Gigi*, I learned that any woman, however awkward and precocious, can learn how to become elegant.

Being *Stylish AF* starts as a mindset that becomes a mood. There are no requirements other than you begin with a mind that is ready to go to work. So, let's get it.

When my clients come to work with me, they expect me to give them a shopping list of must-have items. But I know the real secret sauce to personal style is to ensure that your confidence and body image align with your clothes. We don't just slap a cute outfit on you and leave you with your unstylish and unkind thoughts. We don't start buying a ton of new clothes. The first thing I teach all of my clients is that stylish clothes and a beautiful personal style begin with stylish thoughts. You can have the cutest outfit in the world, but if your thoughts about yourself are janky, you will still feel janky. You must work on your thoughts first. The clothes will follow.

Style is an outward expression of how you think and feel about yourself. When you look in the mirror or see a picture of yourself (without the damn filters), you see yourself as you truly are in that moment. Unlike *Gigi*, we aren't dressing for anyone else—our Auntie's, grandmama, or a man. To be a freaking lady is to dress for yourself.

Since style is for you alone and is an outward expression of your thoughts and feelings, what does your current outfit, clothing, and/or wardrobe say about you? Does it reflect the thoughts and feelings that show how much you love, care, and respect yourself? Or is it more of an outward expression of how janky you've been feeling about yourself. Think janky and dress janky over a period of time, and that becomes your whole personal style.

To go from being janky to *Stylish AF* is all about learning to pay attention to yourself again. I can help you get to *Stylish AF* with the tools I teach in Style School. I use the Jank-o-Meter, a shorthand way of learning where you are currently with your sense of style while teaching you to uplevel in small, manageable baby steps. I will walk you through each marker on the Jank-o-Meter scale.

JANKY

Janky is the lowest starting point. When you think janky thoughts, you are remembering all of the mean-ish stuff you say to yourself daily. Your mind immediately goes to what you think are your flaws. You call yourself fat, disgusting, or gross. You eventually stop looking in the mirror because why even bother. Then, one day, you look in the mirror, or somebody tags you in a picture on Facebook. You are both pissed off and surprised because you didn't know you really looked like that.

When you feel janky and say mean janky things to yourself, you dress accordingly. You don't wear or buy clothes that fit. You've given up. The thought of going into a dressing room makes you want to cry. Then, you start to hold your body hostage. You tell yourself you cannot buy new clothes or nice things until you have reached the perfect weight or size.

Of course, you decide why even bother. You stop caring about how you're dressed. You quit looking in the mirror. You run around thinking, feeling, and looking janky. Style? What style. You no longer believe you even have one.

I've been there. If this is you, I want you to know you are not alone. I am not preaching at you. I'm sitting right next to you, boo; I see you.

In law school, I went through a serious funk. I would sit for hours each day studying. My back ached, and my head hurt most of the time. I ate and ate and ate to stay awake. There was no time to look in the mirror in the morning. I stopped getting dressed. The clothes I had no longer fit me. The few times I tried to get dressed only made me feel worse. I remember I had an internship interview and had to get my booty in gear and put some clothes on. I woke up extra early that morning because even putting a bra on took some mental effort. When I put on my only pair of "good" black pants, I discovered that they barely fit. I got them halfway up my thighs and knew getting them the rest of the way up would require some effort. I pushed and squeezed until I got the button to close.

Then I caught a glimpse of myself for the first time in a long time. Like I really saw myself. I was staring at a stranger whose poor belly was being squished to death by her too-tight pants and had major booby bubbling from a bra that was two sizes too small. I was overheated from the exertion of trying to squeeze myself into these pants. My little face was rounder, redder, and sweatier than I had remembered.

I cannot convey to you the sadness and dismay I felt. Shame wouldn't even begin to cover the feeling I experienced at that moment. All I could do was to unbutton my pants, sit on the edge of my bed with my belly spilling out the top and sides of those pants, and cry.

Not paying attention to my body had finally caught up with me. I had been treating myself like I was all brain and no body. My body finally had my attention. My janky thoughts and feelings about myself and my body lead to a janky ass wardrobe two sizes too small. I couldn't even fathom buying new clothes because I convinced myself that I didn't deserve them at my current weight and size. I was punishing myself for not being some ideal body size. I had refused to look in the mirror for so long that I wasn't even aware of how bad it had all become. I had ignored myself as if I could truly make myself go away and become an amorphous brain without a body.

Eventually, I did seek help. I prayed. I went to a therapist, talked to my law school counselor, and spoke to my pastor. I finally found my life coach and mentor. Over time, my janky thoughts and feelings began to lift. I made my way from janky to good enough, to better than good, to *Stylish AF*. It didn't happen overnight. I didn't chant mantras at myself until I force-fed love down my throat. That is so barfy, and my brain wouldn't have believed me anyway, at least not yet.

Instead, I started to celebrate small wins. I put on a bra. I celebrated. I put on pants that had a button and a zipper. I celebrated. I threw on a cute scarf. I freaking celebrated. It may seem trivial and goofy AF at first, but when you've been feeling janky for so long, every small act of self-care becomes a win.

Once I started to get dressed daily, I began to see things as they really were. I spent more time acknowledging my presence. I noticed that most of my clothes were stained or simply didn't fit. So I got rid of them. Item by item. One by one.

I didn't go out and buy a whole new wardrobe right away because I was broke AF. Nope, I bought a bra that was affordable and fit. It was ok. Just fine. Good enough. Soon after, the pants and shirts followed. Eventually, my janky, old, stained clothing that didn't fit was gone.

After that, I upleveled again. And again, the bras came first.

This time, I bought a better bra. It fit better and was a better quality. Bye-bye, booby bubble. Hello, tata relief! Pants and tops were next. The fog in my head continued to lift. I sometimes had days when I felt janky – I'm human – but they were less frequent, and I had learned to be my own cheerleader.

The last thing I did on my upleveling journey was dial in my sense of style. I knew which brands fit because I had actually gone into a dressing room and tried on clothes. I no longer made allowances for clothes that were just okay or items that happened to be on sale. NO more hand-me-downs that weren't my style. I bought only the best because I could see how different I felt and thought throughout the entire process. It was amazing to start and end the day feeling confident in clothes that fit. I was showing up like a boss because I dressed like one.

I didn't try to replace everything at once. I took baby steps and celebrated the milestones. Did I suddenly discover a long lost rich aunt? Nope. Didn't need one. I remembered the advice of my aunties and mother to "pontes chu-ching." As your professor of glam and elegance, I am dispensing advice and tools for you because most of us don't have a rich aunt to buy us a new wardrobe. You don't need one. You can uplevel all on your own with my favorite tool: the Jank-o-Meter.

The Jank-o-Meter will show you what it looks like to move from janky to elegant – what it looks like to become *Stylish AF*.

Jank-o-Meter to *Stylish AF*

	What you see	What you think	How it feels	How you dress
Janky	When you see a mirror you immediately leave the room and say, "Look in the mirror?! Hell no. There is no point."	You don't think anything in particular about yourself because you refuse to look in the mirror. You try hard not to think about yourself..	You feel like crap. You feel completely defeated.	Your clothes don't fit. They have holes and stains. Or you wear free swag shirts that are too big (so technically they fit).
Good	You give yourself a five-second glance before you run out the door.	You think thoughts like, "I look okay. It will do. Ain't nobody got time to look in the mirror all damn day."	Rushed, hurried, and meh. Not bleh, just meh.	You dress for comfort and practicality. No time for fun or style. Presentable, but no pizzazz.

	What you see	What you think	How it feels	How you dress
Better	You take a longer look. There is some thought to getting ready. You may even smile at your reflection from time to time.	You notice the things about yourself that you actually like. Yeah, this looks good.	Kind and calm. No longer bleh or meh. You start to feel good about what you see.	You are more thoughtful in how you dress and it shows. Items fit. No need to pull or tug on your clothes.
Stylish AF	You take a good long look at your bad self. You smile, wink, and twirl when you see yourself in the mirror.	YASSS BOOO YASSS	Confident	Your style reflects your confidence and your self-love. You are wearing your inner lady boss like a fabulous dress. It shows.

Where are you on the meter?

Where are you on the Jank-o-Meter to *Stylish AF* scale? Do you identify more with Janky, Good, Better, or *Stylish AF*? How do you get from Janky to *Stylish AF*?

Just like I did. Start slow and celebrate small wins along the way. Pay particular attention to whether you are getting ready each day or not.

Do you look in the mirror every day? Are you giving yourself the cold shoulder? Did you say mean things to yourself while looking in the bathroom mirror today? When was the last time you reminded yourself that you are an amazing badass?

That truly is the biggest indicator of where you are on the scale. Don't kid yourself either—good is okay, but you, my darling, can do so much better. Be your own cheerleader. Take the next step to up-level from janky.

For *Stylish AF* to become a mood and a way of life, we must practice often. Just like Gigi did with her Auntie. You can do that for yourself. You can show up for your lady lessons. Even if you start at Janky, you can move to Good, Better, and finally, *Stylish AF*. Start with getting a bra that fits. Spend a little more time in front of that mirror. The rest will follow if you celebrate those small daily wins.

The Clothes

Now that you are familiar with the Jank-o-Meter, I want you to see how it directly applies to up-leveling your wardrobe. As I said, I started with my bras and then my undies. Once you know where you are overall on the Jank-o-Meter scale, see where your bras and undies rank on that same scale. Then, apply the scale to each item of clothing you have until you have up-leveled your wardrobe, style, and mood to *Stylish AF*.

If it has holes or stains, it has to go. If an item doesn't fit, bye-bye. Uplevel to good quality clothes. Eventually, you can work your way to items that are beautiful and perfectly tailored. For example, move from a drawer full of period panties to solid cotton undies that fit, and then to daily lingerie.

Did I start with lingerie? Hell no. I initially upleveled to get some relief and not pick at my undies all day. I was happy when I moved from janky to items that fit and eventually worked my way up to beautiful pieces that I was proud to wear.

My grandmother believed that you should always wear a fresh pair of undies when you go out; a matching bra and undies set would be preferable, of course. Just in case you got into an accident. Heaven forbid the EMT or firefighter should see you in your janky underwear.

Just imagine the emergency personnel rushing in to save your life and needing to cut your clothes off your body. Instead of immediately performing life-saving measures, they pause to evaluate the jankiness of your underwear. Did you meet their standards? Heaven forbid they let you die while they're talking crap about your undies.

While this sounds ludicrous, most of my clients have a drawer full of janky undies and believe that it's ok for them to be janky because, you know, a lady needs a few pairs of period panties. The problem is all of your panties become period panties, and you start to tell yourself that no one is going to see your underwear anyway.

You see your underwear, and your opinion matters more than the opinion of an imaginary fireman. It matters the most. You see yourself in your underwear. You matter—your thoughts about yourself and your underwear matter. So next time you hear yourself tell that lie or make an excuse to wear janky underwear, I want you to think of my grandmother and the hunky firemen. More importantly, I want you to remember that what you see when you look in the mirror and how you feel is what matters most.

Getting to a place where you regularly feel and dress stylish AF starts with the thoughts you think about yourself and your clothing. We often allow too many people or voices in the dressing room with us, and we discount our ability to discern what is janky or stylish. Even worse, we know the difference, and we not only discount ourselves, but we begin to ignore ourselves completely. To get to *Stylish AF* on the regular, you have to be the only person that you get dressed for. You have to decide that you are a good enough reason to get ready. That's why starting with your undies is the perfect measuring test. What state are they currently in? Where are they on the Jank-o-Meter? That will likely tell us the state of the rest of your wardrobe.

Are you resistant to buying new undies or clothes? Or are you like, "Hells yes, I'm at least ready to buy items that fit me. I'm ready to uplevel from janky to good now and then uplevel quality over time."

Let's use that same Jank-o-Meter to evaluate the current state of your undies, and then apply it to your entire wardrobe.

Wardrobe Evaluation	FIT: How does the item fit	QUALITY: Will this item last	FEELING: How do you feel about yourself when you put this item on?
Janky	Butt munchers, droopy drawers, holes, squishing, itching	Itching, elastic is warbly, thinning fabric, low quality, holes and stains	Frustration, defeated, self-loathing, apathetic
Good	The clothes fit, but barely. One big lunch and your belly will hang over the top of your pants	These are your affordable items that come in a pack. Not the best, but definitely not the worst	Meh, bleh, shoulder shrug, neutral
Better	These clothes fit without worrying about eating too much at lunch. There was some thought into how they fit when you purchased them.	You've paid a bit more for these. You may have even purchased each pair individually.	Encouraged, Ready, Prepared
Stylish AF	You put these on and marvel at how they lift your tushy, hug your hips, and grace your belly.	Excellent quality. Time and money were spent in the purchase of these.	Confident, ready to slay and conquer. (You even take that second glimpse in the mirror)

When you purchase clothes going forward, use the same tools to evaluate your wardrobe. Create a *Stylish AF* wardrobe by replacing one item at a time. Be thoughtful about your purchases, and purchase one item at a time. Too often, I see capsule wardrobe lists or lists of must-have items that do not fit my client's personality or lifestyle. Style is personal. Fashion is what is going on outside of you. You get to decide whether to make the latest fashions part of your personal style. Let's look at each of the evaluation criteria used above.

What is the quality of the items in your current wardrobe?

You may have a large number of items in your wardrobe, but are they quality? I have a client who had three full closets, multiple plastic storage containers, and two dresser drawers full of clothes. To many people, it would be amazing to have so many choices, but it became paralyzing for my client. She firmly believed that she had nothing to wear even as she looked through all of her clothes. Why? Because she refused to wear most items because she didn't feel they were high quality.

I'm sure most of you ladies have heard "quality over quantity." But what does that even mean? Other than to prompt you to think, "Yeah, but WTF is quality?" So here are some measuring sticks for quality:

1. Price: This is not an automatic measure of quality, but it can quickly help you determine whether this is an item you intend to use as an undershirt and later cut up for use as a dust rag. (Another shout out to my grandma.)

2. Tactile: Hold the item in your hand. Does it feel nice? Hold it up to the light. Is it transparent? Does it feel itchy? Does it seem like it would cause a crazy static reaction and drive you crazy?

3. Material: Read the tag to see what percentage of this garment is made from natural fibers like cotton, silk, or cashmere? What about rayon or spandex. Natural fibers aren't the only thing you should consider, but you should look at in your quality evaluation.

4 .How was the sucker made? Examine the garment inside and out. Is it lined? Are the seams finished (where two pieces of fabric are sewn together, are they unraveling, or does it look nice and neat)? Does the fabric unravel easily? Are there any skipped stitches or bubbles?

5. Easy-to-spot flaws: Lipstick, foundation, grease, shoes, frayed fabric, and broken zippers.

These are the top five things to look for to determine if an item is a quality item. I also want to pause here and remind you that quality also stands for qualitative. Does this fit your personal style? I can give you all of the damn charts and evaluation guides in the world, but at the end of the day, the most important qualifier is whether you like it.

My client, the one with the three closets, storage containers, and drawers full of clothes, stopped considering whether she actually liked an item. She would buy clothes because they were on sale, included in a package, or given to her. At no point did she ever stop and ask herself if the item met her personal qualifications. Quality is the easy stuff to look for, but more importantly, QUALITY is personal. Does the item meet your personal style qualifiers? If not, then buh-bye. Don't even let that stuff in your house where it will take up space next to items that you actually love.

How do you feel about yourself when wearing the item?

Often in marketing and advertising, too much emphasis is placed on how clothes are supposed to make you feel. This is especially true during the holidays where you are promised that you will feel merry and bright once you buy the perfect dress. Hallmark movies and shows like "Say Yes to the Dress" perpetuate the idea that if only you could find the "right" item, you would automatically feel "right" about yourself too.

Unfortunately, a dress, a pair of jeans, and all the glitter sparkle in the world do not have the power to make you feel good about yourself. It is not your clothes' job to make you love yourself or feel good about yourself. That is your job. Your clothes have no magical capabilities. It is a pile of fabric that has been stitched together. No magic there.

What is powerful and magical is the woman who wears the garment. She is the one with all of the abilities. She has the power to feel good about herself with her thoughts and the feelings she creates from those thoughts. When evaluating items in your current wardrobe or items you are considering purchasing, ask how you feel about yourself when you are wearing the item. Not how you feel about the garment, but how you feel about yourself while wearing it.

I had a client who had a beautiful dress that she loved to look at on the hanger. It was her "goal" item she would wear when she "finally lost the weight." While on her weight loss journey, she walked by the dress every day. It hung in her closet where she could see it. It was a taunting and tantalizing reminder of how she "would" feel when she lost the weight and could finally fit into that dress. She imagined all of the places she would go. Her imagination went wild, envisioning how confident she would feel. It was as if she could hear the tinkling of glasses and feel herself swaying across a dance floor.

When she finally lost enough weight to wear the dress she had idolized for months, she hated it. She didn't suddenly feel confident and sexy when she put it on. The dress didn't magically obtain powers and instill confidence and sexiness within her. Her body was now the size she wanted, but wearing the dress didn't make her feel as good as she had imagined. Those months of feeling confident and sexy in her mind were not wasted, though. She simply didn't know that the power to feel those things always lay within her grasp.

It's like when Dorothy finds out that she always had the power to leave Oz and go home. She went through some crazy stuff and killed two witches at the behest of the craziest witch of them all. (Like really, Gilda, you couldn't tell her in Munchkin Land that she could use the shoes to get home? But, I digress.)

I don't want you to wait months to squeeze your booty into a dress only to be disappointed when you don't suddenly feel a rush of confidence and *Stylish AF*. I want to tell you from the start, at the beginning of the Yellow Brick Road, that you always have the power to feel those things. You always have had and will have the power to make yourself feel good about yourself. NOT because of the dress or the red ruby slippers you're wearing. The garment must conform to you, not you to the garment. When you put the item on, how do you feel about yourself? Does it enhance or detract from how you feel about yourself?

Wearing an ill-fitting garment is often one of the biggest detractors to fostering positive feelings about yourself. Think about how Dorothy would have felt if those ruby slippers had caused blisters or squished her toes? She would've had a hard time following the yellow brick road. First, assess how the garment fits. Then, ask how you feel about yourself in the garment. Feelings encompass physical feelings and mental feelings.

Three Must-Haves for Every Wardrobe

Every wardrobe must have:

1. Undies
2. Clothes
3. Shoes

The most crucial thing these items have in common is that they MUST FIT. You can purchase the most expensive clothing, but it will not matter if it does not fit you. Ill-fitting clothes look terrible and make you feel physically awful, which brings us right back to janky. The price of clothing is never as important as the fit. Fit is everything, my darling.

Think of the woman who wants to dress up, so she pulls out her heels. The ones she still needs to "break in." They were on sale, and she got a great deal. Even though they pinched her toes and dug into her heels, she strolled down the store aisle. Despite the fit issues, she thought she could "break them in." Into her cart and then her closet, the shoes went. Out they came on a morning when she wanted to look her best. What do you think happened to our leading lady when she wore these ill-fitting shoes for an entire day?

After work, she has to walk blocks to her subway stop and down the stairs to get onto the crowded train where she has to further steady her feet for the ride home. All the while, she is wincing and trying to put on a brave face. She knows that if she takes the shoes off to rest her feet for one second, she won't be able to get the damn things back on her feet. Every woman who sees her pities her because they've been there, too. Don't be that woman. Only buy items that fit.

All day, this poor woman was distracted by her tortured feet. The blisters and the shoes digging into her ankles distracted her from her mission in life: to conquer and slay. Instead of being focused on her mission and life's work, she was navigating the streets with aching feet.

Wearing comfortable, properly fitting clothes prevent all-day distractions such as picking at a wedgie, worrying that a janky zipper will slip down and expose your belly, keeping your bra band over your back fat. I had one client that wore a bra two cup sizes too small. Her breast actually popped out and freed itself from the tyranny of a too-tight cup. All the tugging, pinching, and pulling are needless time sucks and distractions from your true mission. Confident women build legacies. They run things. You, my darling, are a future legacy builder. Don't let ill-fitting clothes distract you.

You deserve so much more than a janky pair of undies munching your butt all day. Invest in better undies so you can invest your time in better pursuits. Check to see where your clothing fits on the Jank-o-Meter. Assess and evaluate the quality and fit of your garments. Do not tolerate any clothing distractions.

Why Does Being *Stylish AF* Even Matter?

Being *Stylish AF* requires you to dress in a way that allows you to do your work in the world without distraction. Be willing to invest in the clothes that you show up in to rule the world. Be willing to practice lady lessons even when you have no specific role model to look to. Model the behavior you wish to see most. Do it for you because there is an entire generation of lady bosses waiting in the wings behind you watching your every move and mimicking what you say and do. Become the woman who gives the lessons and models the behavior. Be the woman you needed when you were young. Start with becoming *Stylish AF* and creating a wardrobe in which you can slay and conquer.

Think about superheroes and their wardrobes: They get a call to action and then put on a costume that will help them step into their superhero persona. Superman has a cape; Wonder Woman has her gold cuffs; Catwoman a CatSuit; and Elastigirl a mask. Superheroes wear their costumes when they go out to conquer and slay. What will you wear to a showdown with your goals? Janky undies, holey socks, and stained sweats? Hell to the no! Be it cape or suit, you deserve to show up like the lady boss hero ready to conquer and slay.

Homework

Using the Jank-o-Meter above, determine the current state of your undies.

Using the Jank-o-Meter above, determine the current state of your wardrobe.

List three janky items in your wardrobe that you need to toss.

Where can you uplevel your undies?

Where can you uplevel your clothes?

To take these concepts further, listen to the following episodes of the *Modern Vintage Podcast with Miss J.*

Podcast Episode Guide

Episode 04: A Peek Inside the Undies Drawer

Episode 05: Bra Bra Ooh La La

Episode 23: Fancy on Purpose

Episode 29: Personal Style

Episode 35: Creating a Uniform

Episode 47: 3 Wardrobe Must Haves

Episode 59: Time Travelling Closet

BEAUTY: At Every Size and Shape

I call shenanigans on the old adage, "Beauty is in the eye of the beholder." It makes us beholden to the beholder to decide whether we are beautiful. I say SCREW that. You get to decide you are beautiful. Yours is the only opinion that matters.

You can rally against the ridiculous standards of the beauty industry. The beauty and style industry do not represent the reality of the human spectrum of color, size, shape, or hair texture. While this is true, the beauty and style revolution of more varied representation begins with you. We must always come back to *Do you think you are beautiful?*

We can create systemic shifts in what is considered the current standard of beauty, but at a most basic level – *Do you think you are beautiful?* Don't give me the list of what other people think, say, or compliments you have received. Being a freaking lady will require you to dress for yourself, think for yourself, and set your own standard of beauty.

Lion King Hair

When I was younger, my hair was cut in a straight blunt line across my shoulders. I have naturally curly thick hair, so this caused my hair to jut out from three points on my head. I had a triangular-shaped halo framing my little face and wore giant thick pink glasses with sparkles. It was a glorious 90s-tastic sight to behold. I had a lion's mane.

I was teased about my hair at school and at church. Kids would pull my hair and call me names. One kid even threw gum into my hair, and you can imagine trying to get it out of that mane. To make matters worse, the *Lion King* movie came out around this time. Wherever I went, my singsonging hecklers would follow, and they loved to dig deep and sing, "In the jungle, the mighty jungle…" They even went as far to do the falsetto with a "wheeeee!" You get the drift. I had so much shame around my hair that I started wearing hats. I wore a hat every single day in the fourth grade to try and tame my mane. Eventually, it grew out, but my love of hats remained. Somewhere along all of the sing-song taunting, I started to believe that something was wrong with my hair.

When I was in the sixth grade, I met K and her beautiful cousins. They wore their hair in high top buns and used a brown lacquer gel to lay their baby hairs around their faces in a curlicue frame. I thought they were so cool. I longed to look like them and do my hair like that, too. I thought they were beautiful, and I was convinced that everyone hated my hair.

So these beautiful cousins took on the challenge of coaxing my hair into a smooth top bun. My hair had grown out really, really long by this time, so the top bun was not wisps of hair arranged around a tube sock. Instead, it looked more like a giant halo framing my head. They also did their best to schlack down my baby hairs, but it looked a bit cockeyed. When they finished, none of us were quite sure of the results. I was convinced this was the key to loving my hair. But, hours later, I decided having great hair stacked on my head wasn't worth the pain. So, down it all came.

I think it is fair to say there were gasps and exclamations as my hair cascaded down. For the first time in my life, I heard people all around me saying, "You've got that good hair!" They believed that all Puerto Rican girls were born with "good hair." I had no idea what good hair was, but suddenly, I was in the "good hair" club, which I never imagined I would be a member of. I was unsure why they thought my hair was indeed beautiful when everywhere else I went, it was something akin to a laughable lion's mane. The cousins believed that my hair was beautiful, but I didn't know at the time that I could adopt their belief as my own.

I come from a family of women with all different hair colors and textures. My sisters have beautiful, manageable hair. I firmly believed I did not. As there were no immediate reference points for "good hair" that looked like mine, I held firm to my belief that the cousins, although admirable for their mad hair skills, were wrong about my hair.

Then my nieces were born. They have the most beautiful hair, and each of them has a different texture, color, and length of hair. They are magnificent, and so is all of their hair. I 100% believed that about them, while ignoring all of my hair issues. I could believe it enough for them, but not for me.

Until one day, I went to church with my hair down. It was long, curly, and wild. I had not gone to church like that in over a decade. Don't get me wrong, I would show up rocking a top bun, braids, or a hat, but I never let that wild hair out at church. Then my sweet nieces saw my hair and told me how much they loved it. They were so excited to see me with my hair down. They saw my hair. They saw themselves in my hair. I now saw my history with my hair for what it was...a lame excuse to keep my beauty tamed for fear of what others would think—never considering my most important little audience.

My nieces had never seen my hair down. When I was their age, I was desperate for someone to tell me how beautiful I was and how beautiful my hair was. That I was normal, and so was my hair. I had failed to do that for my nieces. I was not being the woman I needed when I was little. The force of that knowledge hit me profoundly for two reasons.

One, I had committed to believing other people should find my hair beautiful, but when they did, I didn't believe them. I thought the entire world, particularly my classmates and other kids at church, should apologize to me and tell me I was beautiful. I was waiting for the world to do what I was unwilling to do for myself.

Two, I had not done for my nieces what I most needed when I was little: a person who looked like me, or at least similar to me, telling me I was beautiful and didn't need to change a damn thing about my hair. I was not modeling for them a woman who believed she was beautiful and living from that place.

From my nieces, I learned that little humans are watching and mimicking the adults around them. They are looking to you for cues and clues about what beauty is and what is beautiful. You are the one to set the standard of beauty for your family, school, church, workplace, or wherever other humans gather. You set the standard of beauty for yourself and the other little humans that come after you.

Do you believe that you are beautiful? To be a freaking lady, you must set the beauty standard for yourself. Most of us are never taught to set the standard, but are taught to work within a standard and to conform ourselves to that standard. So, how do we go from believing that our hair, size, weight, etc. should be different than it is to believing it is beautiful? How do we go from thoughts like " I hate my hair" or "I hate my body" to "I am beautiful, all of me, just as I am?"

We do the same type of work we did with becoming *Stylish AF.* We must apply the same principles. We work our way up to "I am beautiful, all of me, just as I am." We don't start there and chant it to ourselves like a magical incantation. The truth is that unlearning and relearning new skills like how to think about yourself takes practice. You cannot hate yourself into a place of beauty, and you can't hate your hair from curly to straight.

Meet yourself where you are and then work your way up to a new set of beliefs and standards of beauty. When you set the standard, you raise the standards of those around you.

Beauty as a Given Proof

I'm going to bust out some geometry and logic for you in this section. Bear with me because once you wrap your brain around this, you will never see yourself the same way again. Perhaps it is my training as a lawyer or that I was a mathlete. (Oh hell yes to all the nerdiness. Cutest big-haired mathlete ever!)

In geometry, there are "proofs," which are essentially an argument written down in math form. The proof starts with a basic fact known as a given. Without a given, we don't have much of a math argument. Givens are facts. We start our math argument with a fact, and then we make a series of intermediate conclusions that lead to the final conclusion. Any persuasive writing you may have done in college is based upon this same system of logical argument. You start with givens and work your way to a conclusion. Lawyers are taught to think, write, and speak this way.

Did you know that your beauty is a given? It is not the final conclusion of an argument. It requires no proof through anecdotes, your facial symmetry, skin color, or booty size. Your beauty needs no defending. It needs no explanation. It simply is a given. When we begin the conversation with the premise that your beauty is given, it takes the pressure off you to conform to what other people look like or what you believe other people think is beautiful.

When we begin with the premise that your beauty is an absolute given, beauty is no longer a competition or a comparison game. You get to be the you-est you there ever was because there is no comparison. That is literally impossible. There is only one of you. We cannot take your beauty at the top of the proof and compare it to others. That would be illogical. Your given beauty is a given.

Let's use an apple as an example. It's a type of fruit called an apple. We don't question its apple-ness. We accept that and let it be its apple self. Now, there are matters of taste and preferences amongst the apple strains. Someone may like the taste of a very sweet apple, while someone else may prefer the bitter bite of a granny smith. It doesn't mean something is fundamentally wrong with the sweet apple for being sweet. We wouldn't require it to shed its skin, turn green, and make itself sour to become a granny smith. Nope, that would be weird. Instead, we allow it to be its sweet apple self. We accept that as a given.

The funny thing about apples is that we make room for taste and preferences. We don't make it mean anything about the apple. The green granny smith isn't referred to as the "poor green granny smith" and looked at with pity or derision because it is green. It's green-ness is a given, not a matter to be pitied or changed. We expect that people who like those apples are showing a matter of preference or taste. We don't make it mean anything about them either. Although I am sure there is some random BuzzFeed quiz somewhere asking you what kind of apple you are.

When you are an apple, and your apple-ness is a given, and the rest is a matter of taste, there is nothing to worry about. You get to be your apple self. The same is true of humans. We come in all shapes, colors, and sizes. Our beauty as a human being is a given. The rest is a matter of taste and preference. It requires you to do nothing but enjoy your own version of sweetness or greenness. None of it means that there is something wrong with you that requires you to change or conform yourself to be like the next apple on the shelf. That would be absurd. We don't require that of apples, and we certainly should stop requiring that of ourselves and the other women around us.

How To Believe You Are Beautiful Just As You Are

Believing you are beautiful just as you are is a simple practice that requires a lot of practice. I don't advocate that you stand in front of a mirror and chant beauty incantations at yourself repeatedly. If you don't believe them, it is like trying to force-feed yourself the nastiest boiled vegetable you can think of that has gone cold and congealed. The second it hits your tongue, your gag reflex is activated, and you want to vomit. Next time, you tell yourself, "Oh, but it's so good for you." Your brain literally remembers that the last time you tried it, you felt like barfing.

This is a very condensed version of what is happening in your brain. When you shout mantras at yourself that you don't believe, your brain's gag reflex is activated. Then the negative thoughts that you believe to be true come up like that automatic gag reflex. While it is lovely to know that believing you are beautiful will ultimately be good for you, let's ease you into this belief.

Beliefs are ideas we get from our past that we have thought about long enough to take on the idea as true. Like my hair story. I believed my hair was ugly, should be straight, and blonde. I was teased about my hair, which only reinforced my thoughts about my hair. I took my thoughts about my hair and gathered evidence from my tormentors that something was wrong with my hair and created an entire belief system about my hair. Even when others told me the exact opposite, I didn't consider it as true because I literally could not believe it. It would have shaken my belief about myself. Nope, I was committed to my hair story and the belief backed by all of the evidence I found to support it.

The same thing happens to many of my clients. What started as a passing thought like "I feel fat" coupled with a tag size that created evidence to support that thought turned into the belief that "I am fat and there is something wrong with me." Even when there is contra-dictory evidence that somebody thinks your current size or weight is beautiful or perfect, or you learn that your current weight is someone else's "goal weight," it does not matter. You now see signs that there is something wrong with the size of your body.

Step back and consider all of the thoughts you have about your body. Write them down. Look at them. AND, most importantly, start to evaluate and examine where the hell they originated. What current evidence are you using to support thoughts and cementing them into beliefs?

You get to decide whether you want to change those thoughts and beliefs or keep them – no matter how old those thoughts may be. It is important to stop and evaluate them because those thoughts about your weight, size, body, and hair are the foundation of the beauty standard you are setting for yourself, your family, and your community.

If you believe that the beauty and style industry needs to be more inclusive, cool. But are you being inclusive when it comes to how you look? Does your personal beauty standard include people that look like you? Are you accepting and kind towards yourself? Do you believe that all bodies are good bodies, including yours? Check yourself and the stories you have committed to believing.

Believing new ideas requires you to commit to practicing a new story in your head and having answers for the old stories when they resurface. And they will. For example, when I first began my journey to change my thoughts about myself, I hated my hair, and I especially hated my body. (I was much thinner when I began this work, so I can tell you for sure that big or small, I had mental work to do.) I created stories upon stories to illustrate why my self-hating thoughts were 100% accurate. All of those old thoughts merged to create a story about myself, which became my beliefs.

I started practicing new thoughts the way I thought I **should**. You know, repeating stuff I didn't believe to myself over and over and over again in the mirror. I hoped that this would do the trick. Usually, I just walked away feeling worse because the crap I was saying to myself was drowned out by the louder noise of my old beliefs.

Then, I found life coaching and learned why that mantra repeating crap was not working, no matter how precisely I uttered the same words to myself. It was like trying to cross all of the monkey bars in one fell swoop. I would never make it to the end of the row of bars. It was as though I was hyperextending my shoulder socket only to fall knees first into the sand pit below. That is what is happening when you beat yourself over the head with a thought you aren't quite ready for yet. You hyperextend yourself and land knees first. It hurts like hell. The worst kind of hurt, too—heart hurt. I will teach you a more effective way to unlearn old thoughts and beliefs and slowly create new thought patterns that will eventually become new beliefs.

We must begin slowly. One monkey bar at a time, until we have gathered enough strength and agility to swing from one rung to the next one. Eventually, we will find ourselves at the end of the monkey bars. Think of grabbing that last rung as finally believing "I love my-self, all of me, just as I am."

For now, practice new tiny thoughts about yourself that are more believable.

Breadcrumb Thoughts

Let's say "I am beautiful" is the Candy Land Castle on the Candy Land game board. You want to get to the castle and show up your sister, who you know cheats at every board game. The new thought you want to practice is several spaces away from where you are now. There is no jumping 20 squares ahead. The color cards don't allow for that.

In Candy Land, you move towards Candy Lane Castle, one colored square at a time. Sometimes you get the purple square card and are forced to retreat a few steps back; such is life. That "I am beautiful" thought is approachable when you move one square at a time. We start at the first square with whatever thought or thoughts we are cur-rently thinking about ourselves. If you say things to yourself like "I hate my body" or "I hate my hair," that is your starting square. Your next thought is slightly better than your starting point thought. It looks a bit like this:

I hate my body (Starting Point)

I have a body

This is a human body

This is what a human body looks like

Other human bodies look like this

It is possible that I can like this human body

It is possible that I can like my body

I can like my body

I will like body

I do like my body

It is possible that I can love my body

I can love my body

I do love my body

I love my body (Candy Land Castle)

Use this same methodology with thoughts like "I am ugly" to get to "I am beautiful." You can break it down even further than I did. The goal is to find your starting place on the proverbial game board. Some of you will start with, "I can like my body." Others will have to break it down to something very non-charged like, "It is possible that I can like my body." We are not judging where you begin. The first goal is to find your starting square.

Practice each new thought every day, and look for evidence that it is true. You will notice it takes a lot of effort at first until, over time, you are ready for a new thought along Candy Land Lane. Redirect your brain when it only sees evidence that your old thought was true.

How will you know when you are starting to believe the thought you have chosen to practice? You will begin to feel a sense of ease when you think about it, "Like yeah, duh, I totally can like my body." Then you are ready to practice the thought in the next colored square. It will be uncomfortable again. Some days you will feel like you are on a roll ready to take on new colored squares. Other days it will feel like you are back at square one. The goal is to keep showing up for yourself and stay in the game.

Remember, you are setting new standards of beauty. You are taking down strongholds of thoughts, beliefs, and stories about yourself and the ladies who came before you. This is not light-hearted work. You are doing some hero's work. When you go about setting new standards of beauty, expect the external and internal push back. Your inner voice will require all of your courage and bravery first.

What Do You Do With The Old Thoughts?

Practicing new thoughts is not automatic, and it doesn't mean that your old thoughts are going to magically disappear. Initially, you will have both thoughts at the same time. I will practice the thought, "It is possible that I can like my body," but still think my old thought, "But I really don't like my body. Have you seen my saggy booty…?" Then the internal argument starts in your head. You may even think you've gone nuts because you are having all of this inner dialogue about why your new thought is BS and completely unbelievable.

Some of us plunge headfirst into thinking new thoughts and believe we need to throw away our old thoughts immediately, or that somehow we are doing this transformation journey all wrong because the old thoughts decided to rear their ugly little heads. Your old thoughts are fighting to stay alive, and all you want to do is take care of them with a bucket and a shovel. If only it were really that easy.

So here is what I want you to know, and what I wish I had known when I started to boss up and uplevel my mindset. It feels like total crap at first. You may feel the exact opposite of beautiful, and that is a beautiful thing.

When people say beauty is pain, and they are talking about doing some torturous beauty or diet routine to your body, I think they are partly right. Suddenly believing you are beautiful when you haven't for such a long time will feel very painful. The beauty and diet torture are unnecessary. I want you to know that there is a light at the end of the tunnel. It does get a little easier. Have some compassion and grace for yourself.

We teach toddlers the alphabet one letter at a time. We teach them to count to ten one number at a time. We work our way from number one to number ten, and it is a triumph when it happens. Have the same compassion as you would for a toddler singing their ABCs or 1s through 10s. We don't harangue them for mixing up L,M,N,O,P, and we don't mock them when they jump from three to five.

I don't have you start at 10 and Z and chant those to yourself over and over again. You wouldn't learn the alphabet or how to properly read that way. You would never learn to do algebra if you don't have a basic understanding of the numbers one through 10. Getting to Z or 10 is not what matters most; it's the numbers and letters on the way.

So, my darling, start slowly and with a ton of grace. Begin at whatever your 1 or A is and expect that some days you will shoot for a 5 only to forget 4 and need to start again. There will be days when you feel like uttering 1 or A is a huge effort, then there will be days where you blaze on through to Z. Your brain is creating new neural pathways, just like a toddler learning numbers and letters. Do so with kindness, patience, and grace.

Why Even Try to Change Your Thoughts?

Why even try to change your thoughts? Because every single woman sets the standard of beauty for herself, her family, and her community. It starts with you. If you believe in inclusivity, then it starts with you. If you can't muster the lady balls to keep working until you believe, think of the little humans around you who are watching and mimicking your every move. They are looking to you to set a new standard of beauty. Do it for them.

Don't let "beauty at every size, shape, and color" be another BS mantra we hashtag each other. We shouldn't live in the loneliness of our own heads or the quiet of our bathrooms when we step out of the shower. Allow it, with practice over time, to become a belief that you take action on every day. Action sounds so sexy, right? We can picket and rally, but can we stop and say kind things to ourselves when we glimpse our naked booties in the mirror? I'm asking you to start a beauty standard revolution within your head.

A woman who believes, nay knows, she is beautiful shows up like a boss. She owns her future. She presents differently. Her looks are not a distraction to her. Believe me, hating yourself is a distraction from the real work you were put on this earth to do. A woman who believes she is beautiful models that for the women around her. She shows up with that unquantifiable something. The belief radiates outward and affects all who come into contact with the phenomenon that she is.

What You Say And What You See

Believing you are beautiful is not only what you say to yourself, but also filtering what you take in visually. I worked with a client who we will call "Miss H." When Miss H came to me, she told me she was recommitting to taking care of herself. She had just finished graduate school and was starting a new job. This was going to be her year. She began, as most of us begin, with a new diet and exercise regimen. She was crushing it in the gym and was slaying at work, too. This girl was getting after it. From her outward appearance, she looked like she *should* have felt like she was slaying.

Miss H would bust her butt at work all day, and then she would hit the gym. For Miss H, going to the gym required a certain amount of courage. She would gear up in the bathroom stall. She would avoid the women taking booty selfies in the mirror, put in her earbuds, and get after it. When she concentrated only on herself, she felt like she could conquer the world. There is nothing like a post-workout adrenaline high to make you feel like you can do anything. You want to hold court right up in the gym. That treadmill is your throne.

Then she would bust out her phone.

The comparison would start.

Her fitspo idols on Instagram didn't look like the body staring back at her in the mirror. Her booty had not suddenly transformed into a perfectly sculpted peach. The rolls underneath her sports bra didn't suddenly shrink. Every feeling of sweet, conquering goodness would melt away. Where was her feeling of amazingness now? Was it an apparition? That disconnect from the way she was feeling to what she saw in the mirror is one of the worst feelings in the world. It is beyond disappointment.

Miss H came to me initially to work on her new work style. I love a good work wardrobe but needed to know where her thoughts about herself were before we plunged full steam ahead into dressing her. I understand the power of clothing, and I also know that I could put the loveliest outfit on a client, but if their thoughts about themselves are janky, they will still feel janky.

I had her record her thoughts in a download diary for me for one week. This allowed me to see where she was, but of more import, it helped her to really see where she was. We both noticed the pattern emerge – there was a mix of feelings post-gym. There was a momentary high followed by crestfallen disappointment once she looked in the mirror. She thought for sure something was wrong with her because how could she feel so good one minute and want to cry the next? We talked through what she was thinking, and what she was doing and seeing post-workout.

The problem was definitely NOT with her body. The issue wasn't that she busted out her phone post-workout. We found that her visual diet wasn't matching her new commitment to health and self-love. She was not looking at images of women who looked like her. Her visual interest had no variety of colors, shapes, or sizes. It was one type of woman with no representation for the rest of the shapes, sizes, and colors. The body type she looked at on social media was so different from her own that it was no wonder she was feeling crestfallen and disappointed. Not to mention the work of complete fiction that is some people's Instagram feeds. They can appear lovely, but they aren't reality.

When you start a new diet or a self-love regimen, do you also clean up your visual diet? We are taught to color our plates with fruits and veggies of all different colors when eating healthy. Variety is the spice of life and part of a healthy food plan. We don't treat our visual input the same way. Our visual diets are typically bland. Are we making room on our proverbial plates for all of the colors and varieties? Are all body types, shapes, and colors welcome on your visual plan?

When we have a bland visual diet, it is difficult to see the woman reflected at us as beautiful. We make no room for ourselves on the table. I did this work with Miss H, and I have walked hundreds of other women through the same process in my body image makeover course. We work together to recognize and monitor the thoughts they have about their bodies AND the images they are taking in, and determine whether those images comport with what they see in the mirror.

Usually, there is a disconnect because we aren't used to seeing, or so much as celebrating, a variety of shapes, colors, and sizes in body types. This is especially hard for women who avoid the mirror or having their pictures taken. They are a surprise to themselves, and those glimpses in the mirror at the gym can be devastating, but it doesn't have to be that way. It's just time to clean up that visual diet.

There is a simple way to get started, and it doesn't require you to unfollow or unfriend anyone. We need those women, too, if we are going to have variety in our visual diet. Instead, focus on adding social media accounts that show a diversity of sizes, colors, and weights. Look for women who look like you and the women in your family. Make room for women who are the polar opposite of your weight, color, and size spectrum. Add in some ladies that are only a few places from where you think you want to be on your journey with your body. Finding a variety may seem like a bit of work, but your brain will thank you for it in the long run.

Over time, your brain becomes acclimated to seeing natural bodies and a diversity of body types, so when you look at yourself in the mirror in all of your post-workout or post-shower glory, you will not be surprised at what you see. When we acclimate our brain to seeing bodies that are not perfectly posed or filtered, then we normalize how people in the real world look as opposed to ONLY seeing a particular type of filtered woman on Instagram. More importantly, spend time getting to know your face and body in the mirror so that you think you are beautiful. That is where we began this chapter. Do you think you are beautiful? It's okay if the answer is not "Yes" yet. Use the work in this chapter to help you move to a place where you can believe it is possible and then one day believe.

Homework

Find where you are on the beauty belief map.

What thoughts do you currently think about your beauty? Weight? size?

List the thoughts that you will begin practicing.

Find places you can look for evidence to support the new thought you are practicing.

What little humans do you have in your life, and how will you model this new standard of beauty for them?

Write your new standard of beauty.

Podcast Episode Guide

Episode 03: How to Love Your Body

Episode 17: The After Picture Fallacy

Episode 32: Self Love For Realsies

Episode 54: Not Good Enough

Episode 53: I Don't Feel Beautiful

Episode 52: I Feel Fat

Episode 67: Visible Belly Outline

Episode 66: How to Love Yourself an Eyelash at a Time

ELOCUTION: How to Say Things and Knowing When to Shut Your Glam-Hole

Elocution is the art of clear and expressive speech. I think this is an essential skill for becoming a freaking lady. If you went to charm school in the 1950s, you would have had lessons in elocution, and I believe it should still be taught.

Miss J's Charm School elocution lessons definitely include how to say things and, more importantly, when to shut your glam-hole. This is not your grandmama's charm school, so we will not make you say "red leather, yellow leather" repeatedly. I will not ask you to read Shakespeare aloud. We will examine the basic principle that conversation is a courtesy, and you'll learn how to conduct yourself like a leading lady and not fawn over an insecure male speaker.

Many women have entered the workforce since the Charm Schools of the 40s and 50s. We want more than a seat at the table. We want to own and build the table, too. Whether you own the table, your business, or have a seat at someone else's table, you must learn how to say things and when to just shut your face. Your seat at the table was hard-won and pre-warmed by many women who came before you. Make your Mama and Grandmama proud by acting like a freaking lady now that you have a seat at the proverbial table.

A freaking lady doesn't make it all about her. She knows that conversation is a courtesy. The others at the table are not her friends. She has learned when to inflect a well-placed curse word and when to stay silent.

My grandmother had the skills, but she wasn't allowed a seat at the table. In the fifties, she was an accountant, travel agent, and she owned a traveling baseball team. One of my favorite photos of her shows her sitting in a chair surrounded by a group of people, holding a newspaper in her lap with a headline that translates to, "An exceptional woman." Indeed she was. In addition to her resume, she was also a poet. Her laugh was infectious. I imagine she stood up from that chair arms outstretched busting out her famous isms and telling colorful jokes like the one about the guy with the farting dog under his chair. I imagine a group gathered around her soaking in her charisma and her eloquence. My grandmother could attract people and connect them even though she lived in an era where her skin color and gender made those qualities seem like a rarity.

My grandmother pre-warmed the seats at the table for all the women in my family. This magnificent woman had the *Gift of Gab* and the brains to match her wit. While your grandmother may not have been the same, the idea of a pre-warmed seat is still true for all women. Imagine all of the gifted, charismatic women who came before you. Imagine the black-and-white snapshots of them coming to life. Their passions, worries, and hopes. What we say and do going forward matters. You won't get to meet all the women you are making space for or carving a path for in the future. But one day, some woman will see a picture of you. She will animate you in her mind and imagine your charisma and elocution. You get to decide whether you will also be a Woman of Excellence. Once you have a seat, you get to choose how you show up at the table, what you say, and how you say it.

Conversation as a Courtesy

The most important thing you need to know when learning to speak like a lady is that what's going on in your brain affects what comes out of your mouth. Think about a time when you felt awkward during a conversation. Your face feels hot and, suddenly, your hands feel huge and you don't know where to put them. You keep thinking about where to put your damn hands. "Crossed? No – that's weird and closed off. Behind your back? In your pockets? Even weirder. Ugh!"

Then you remember a person is talking to you. You try to turn your attention back to the conversation. Making eye contact now requires even more effort. There is a moment where you just stare at their eyebrows. Then there is an attempt to at least appear interested with a little nod. However, they just told you their dog died. You're trying to stay focused, but your hands feel even bigger now. Then the person across from you starts rubbing their nose. Now you have it in your brain that you have a booger. Why didn't this person just tell you? You've completely lost focus on the person across from you.

The other person can tell you've completely lost interest. Your eyes are darting back and forth. For a moment, they swore you were staring at their eyebrows. They start to think they have something on their face. They begin to rub their nose and then their eyebrows believing you are trying to send a signal. They keep moving their hands. Now neither of you can stop rubbing your noses, and you both feel awkward and are praying that this torturous interaction ends.

This type of situation happens when conversation is not a courtesy and you get all in your head. The first thing to note is it's not about you, boo. In a conversation, four things are occurring all at once. A lot is going on in each moment, and if we are hyper-focused on ourselves, we will miss three of those four things. The experience is not only awkward for you, but also for the person interacting with you.

While I was living in London, I worked as an intern at a British charity. I answered phones and communicated with other Branch offices of the charity about upcoming events. My very chirpy Californian American accent would call people all over the United Kingdom. It was amusing to hear their surprise that an American was on the other end of the line. To me, everyone else had an accent, not me. My arrogance reached its peak when I had to call someone in Scotland.

A lovely sounding baritone voice answered the phone. I could discern that he had said, "Hello" before I went straight into my whole spiel about why I was calling. I needed some important information before a deadline. I kept talking and talking. I didn't let him speak for several minutes. When this poor man was finally allowed to speak, I couldn't understand a single word he was saying. It was English, but my ear wasn't tuned to his accent, so I couldn't make out what he was saying. If I had let him speak initially, I would have realized this early on in the conversation.

After nodding my head for several minutes (which he couldn't see), I had to put my ego aside and let him know, "I have absolutely no idea what you just said." I then proceeded to tell this gentleman that I was sorry, and it must be my accent. I immediately realized how condescending that sounded and wanted to melt right into my chair. I waited for a few seconds to see if his voice had registered lower in response to my weird blunder. Nope.

He started laughing. It was an incredible deep belly laugh. All I could make out after that was, "my accent …" more laughter. He turned out to be a really kind man. We decided to communicate through email so we could understand each other. I was able to give him a good laugh, and I got the information I needed from him. I also ate a little bit of much-needed Humble Pie.

I took away several things from that interaction. One, it is okay to say, "I don't know" or "I don't understand." Two, coming into a conversation with an arrogant mindset is bound to lead to miscommunication. Three, what you say and what you mean can be different. Finally, what you say and what the other person made it mean can be different.

I Don't Know or I Don't Understand

"I don't know." Those three powerful words are the most common denominator amongst all humans. There will always be something you don't know. There will always be another person who knows more or understands better than you do. In my case, I literally had no idea what he was saying. I didn't understand. Allowing myself to say it was 100% okay.

"I don't understand. Can you please explain further?" It is 100% okay to say that. You know why? Because the person across from you has had the same experience and likely wants you to understand or at least be able to hear what they are saying. It is perfectly normal not to understand or know everything.

Although information is available at our fingertips, we aren't required to enter into every conversation knowing and understanding everything under the sun. Just because we can know things doesn't mean we will always understand or that it won't take time to grasp a concept fully.

Here is the thing, though. When you pretend to know or understand something that you don't, you get the exact opposite of what you want. You often end up in the position that you were trying to avoid. In the case above, I was trying to be cute with my little Californian accent. I was making it all about me and talking and talking and talking. The result was that I came across as kind of an ass, particularly with my accent comment. When my Scottish counterpart began talking, if I was actually listening to him, I would have been able to say, "I am sorry, but I am having trouble understanding you on the phone." No harm, no foul. No weird comments about each other's accents. Then, we could have more quickly gotten to a place where we were communicating. Those emails could have been sent so much faster. Lucky for me that the guy on the other end of the call had a great sense of humor.

The same is true of conversation in person, text, or email. Saying "I don't know" or "I don't understand" creates an opportunity to be understood. Don't pretend that you know or understand something the other person is telling you when you don't.

Save yourself the embarrassment of being called out later. People know when you are pretending or not being entirely truthful. Think back to conversations you had when somebody pretended to understand you or listen, but it was obvious to you they were not. Don't try to be slick. You're not fooling anybody.

Save everyone the time and yourself the embarrassment. A well-placed "I don't know" and/or "I don't understand" can be very useful. Don't hesitate to say it as soon as it is apparent that you do not understand. A lady doesn't waste her time pretending to be someone else or to know something that she doesn't. She does not waste time pretending to understand something she does not understand. She has no time for that. She is willing to take the time to learn more and ensure she better understands.

Learning to pause the conversation and let the other person know that I didn't understand has saved my booty on many occasions, particularly during negotiations. It is disarming to the other side when you stop and ask them to explain their position so you can better understand and relay the information to your client. I can assume I know what you are advocating, or I can stop, ask, and confirm what your position is, or at least so much as you are willing to let me know. There is a time and place to argue and fight, but you would be able to produce a better argument or leverage your position if you actually knew what the other person was arguing or advocating. You may even be on the same page, but have been going around in circles because no one stopped to admit they didn't understand and needed further information or explanation.

It is crucial to debunk the myth that we have to go in bigger, better, stronger, and be more intelligent than our counterparts at the proverbial table. I am all for being prepared; however, I have also realized that there is strength in stopping to listen, being quick to ask questions, and showing a calm confidence when admitting you need further information or explanation. If the other person becomes exasperated, then that is their issue to work through. They are speaking so that others will hear the sound of their voice instead of communicating to be understood. You came to communicate. If others come only to talk and talk, that will quickly become apparent, and there is nothing you can do for those folks. But you don't have to become one of them.

A lady leaves a legacy. She models behavior for the women around her. When she is strong, confident, and willing to say, "I don't know" or "I don't understand," that opens the door for the other people to feel safe in saying it. When you speak, you make space for the women next to you. You become a seat warmer at the proverbial table.

What Is Going On Here?

Conversations are not the exchanges that we believe they are. The sooner we learn this, the better we become at navigating all of the conversations that come with being a freaking lady.

Listed below are the four parts of a conversation, and I will explain each in detail. This knowledge has been life-changing for me and something I've worked on with my clients when they have a "miscommunication."

1. What you say
2. What you mean
3. What they heard
4. What they made it mean

Have you ever wondered how someone heard what you said, but they still are royally pissed at you? They can repeat what you said verbatim back to you, but they made it mean something other than what you intended. They changed the context of your words and vice versa. You may have *said* one thing, but in your head, you really *meant* something else. Conversation can be tricky business when we are not acting like ladies because oftentimes we choose to misinterpret or infer the most negative interpretation rather than evaluate all four versions of the conversation as potentially true.

For example, I knew a woman named R, who had a very aggressive energy. She was blunt and demanding. It was fun to watch her in meetings sizing people up and then cutting them down—until all that energy was focused on me. Before then, I thought she was amazing and an oh-so-talented negotiator. I complimented her for being a woman who knew what she wanted. I had really positive thoughts about her, but that was, of course, before I believed I somehow upset her. Now that all of those skills were directed at me, I was no longer feeling R so much.

I filtered everything she said through my own insecurities. One day she asked for a document, and I heard, "I need this document, *right now.*" I made it mean she thought I was stupid and that she was a total B. Dude, R probably just wanted the freaking document. I noticed myself sending snarky messages along with the document when I emailed them to her. Then, I would live in fear that she would call me out for being snarky. She eventually did.

Not everything everyone says has a hidden meaning. Start with the premise that people say words, and you hear the words. The rest is all interpretation usually filtered through a lens like insecurity, fear, worry, or doubt. It is human to interpret everything as negative.

Knowing that the same set of words can have four different interpretations can help you move through the various conversations and separate fact from fiction. Fact is the actual words that were spoken: "I need this document." Fiction is my interpretation that it was said in a bitchy way with an implied demand that I send the document *right now.* In this scenario, who is really being the B? The woman who asked for a document or the snarky replier? Check yourself, boo, because that B may sometimes be you.

If this is you and you can see yourself interpreting every conversation or words that come your way through a negative lens, I have some good news. You can learn how to converse with courtesy by learning to separate fact from fiction in all of your conversations.

You need to listen, and not just so you can formulate a witty response – so that you can hear the actual words spoken. The manner and the tone are matters of interpretation. In-person or telephone conversations don't include emojis signaling how you feel or create meaning. Your brain has to do all of the work – give it the chance to do that. It is imperative that you stop and listen from the outset so that you get into the practice of separating fact from fiction, actual words spoken versus interpretation of those words. It is more effective to listen from the outset.

Remember, not everyone you come across is your peer. So the chance of you having a communication mishap is more likely, especially since the workforce is made up of so many different generations. Not everyone wants to be your friend, and you don't have to be everyone's friend either.

Leading With Arrogance (Learning When To Shut Your Face)

Leading a conversation with arrogance usually ends with a lesson in knowing when to shut your face. I'm sure you have encountered a person who is a "one-upper," also known as a boar. My family calls them "story-stealers." These are the people who did it better, longer, and faster, and don't listen when you speak. They continually plan what they will say next and when to interject their more colorful story.

I am sure we have all encountered these people or maybe have been one of these people. I have, at times, acted this way, too. It is so embarrassing to admit that, but I want to lead by example. I admit that I too have been a complete and total boar. What about you? Are you a one-upper? A story-stealer?

A freaking lady does not one-up or story-steal the conversation. She does not make it all about her. She doesn't need to. She is not out to impress or delight anyone except herself. One-upping and story-stealing come from a need to impress others because you are not truly impressed with yourself. If you were already impressed with your own accomplishments and self-satisfied, there would be no need to one-up. There would only be a mutual exchange of communication and ideas. Sharing a well-told story and a willingness to listen to others is truly what conversational art is all about. Show respect by truly listening without pretending to hear so you can pause the conversation by interjecting a clever anecdote. You don't need to go there when you're secure in yourself.

This brings me to the second kind of arrogant conversant – the prattler. A prattler is an insecure person who prattles on and on and then insists on telling you just one more thing after you have politely indicated your need or desire to leave the conversation. This kind of person will set up shop in your office, will email, text, or call to ask you a needless array of questions based on hypotheticals. No matter what advice you give them, they will slightly alter the facts in hopes of altering your advice. I'm sure we have all been guilty of being the prattler.

I become a prattler when I am around people I admire or I believe they know more than me. I can feel the motor in my mouth ramp up and take off. Sometimes it feels as if my mind has completely lost touch with my tongue.

As a new attorney, I felt helpless and became an incessant prattler when I would ask for help from a more experienced attorney. Because I was so insecure in my own thought process, I would second-guess others' thought processes. This is a different type of arrogance wherein you are admitting your lack of knowledge and experience, while also questioning the advice, wisdom, or experience of the person in front of you.

I'm discussing the prattler in the arrogant conversation section for a reason. Many people who have this tendency make the conversation all about them and their nervousness. They are like the awkward conversant who focuses on his body language, but the prattler is only concerned about saying everything they have to say whether the other person wants to hear it or not. They are overly concerned with speaking, but they don't listen. They are discourteous. Even when they get a response, they typically don't like it because it doesn't help assuage their fears.

If you are a prattler, just stop and breathe, boo. Stop talking. Don't be like me on the phone with the Scottish guy. Give the other person a chance to hear, listen, and decide whether they want to stay or leave the conversation. Offer the courtesy of an out; nobody likes being trapped in a prattler conversation. When you slow down or stop talking, you allow your brain to shift focus to the other person. Conversation is courtesy first. Sometimes it requires you to shut your face. So, do yourself and everyone else a favor; if you catch yourself doing this, stop. Take a breath. Really look at the other person or refocus your brain by concentrating on the words they're actually saying. Allow them time and space to speak. Consider that they may want to exit the conversation and graciously allow that to take place. You cannot force a conversation. You cannot actually get someone to make you feel better by giving you the "right answer."

Sending back-to-back text messages or emails is just another form of prattling. My mother refers to it as someone *humping your leg*, which provides an immediate visual of a yappy dog in heat humping a stuffed toy, then setting its sights on your leg. You can't really kick the dog, but how freaking annoying. Don't go humping people's legs by prattling on and on without giving them an out. They are not your stuffed toys to hump at your leisure.

A freaking lady doesn't go around humping anyone's leg. She has the wherewithal to stop herself and shift her focus back to the other person or people. She knows it is okay to shut her face and breathe. She graciously accepts when someone wants an out of the conversation because she knows that she will encounter a prattler and want out at some point in the future. She will know when to press for an answer and actually listen to the response given. She can step back and evaluate the information that she is receiving. She has no shame and knows that it's okay not to know something. She is not afraid to ask meaningful follow-up questions because she will actually stop to listen to the answers offered. She will model how to handle situations with grace and understanding. This woman wears a fabulous cape, but her superpower is courteous conversation.

Cursing

Before we sign off, I want to discuss where cursing fits in with the concept of conversation as a courtesy. How does one curse courteously? The key is to know your audience and evaluate your reasons for cursing in the first place. Courtesy has two definitions. The first is concerned with refined manners and gallantry. To be courteous is to be "marked by polished manners, gallantry, or ceremonial usage of a court." While we are concerned with polished manners here, the polished manners come from having self-control and discipline over what flies out of your mouth, as opposed to being born into a certain class of persons. I am more concerned here with the second definition.

To be courteous is to be "marked by respect for and consideration of others." Now, we certainly have no control over other people's perceptions of us. However, we do have control over our self-perception and, in turn, this will affect how we present ourselves and how we treat others. A courteous curse takes into account your respect and consideration for others, while also considering your version of polished manners.

The Supreme Court of the United States in *Miller v. California* developed a three-prong test for obscenity: In his majority opinion,

Chief Justice Warren Burger[1] outlined what he called "guidelines" for jurors in obscenity cases. These guidelines are the three prongs of the Miller test:

(1) whether the average person applying contemporary community standards[2] would find the work, taken as a whole, appeals to the prurient interest;

(2) whether the work depicts or describes, in a patently offensive way, sexual conduct specifically defined by the applicable state law; and

(3) whether the work, taken as a whole, lacks serious literary, artistic, political or scientific value.[3]

Now I am not suggesting you engage in such a rigorous test when you evaluate the merits of a well placed F*ck or another curse word. However, I am suggesting that there is something twofold to consider in whether your cursing is courteous — the community standards (other people) and the power you give to the words you speak (you).

Let's begin with the former—other people. When conversation truly is a courtesy, you will consider the audience with whom you are exchanging words and ideas. Not because you need to change who you are to suit other people, but ultimately do you want to get your message and views across to the other person? Do you want them to hear what you are saying and listen? Knowing your audience is key because a well-timed f*ck could be just the thing needed to convey your message, capture attention, and emphasize key points. However, it could also have the opposite intended effect, turning off your listener and shutting down the communication altogether. A well-timed

---

[1] https://mtsu.edu/first-amendment/article/1325/warren-burger
[2] https://mtsu.edu/first-amendment/article/901/community-standards
[3] Miller v. California, 413 U.S. 15 (1973)

f*ck is different than calling someone a f*ck, so, common sense should rule the day here.

The words you speak have power. Lawyers use words to persuade people. Salespeople use words to persuade people. C-suite executives spend most of their time using words to lead and persuade people. Our words have power not because we can actually change anyone's minds, but because the interpretations and meaning others assign our words have the power to change their minds. This goes back to the concept that every conversation has four parts. So, consider your role in that interplay when a curse word enters your brain and comes out of your mouth. Consider the other party when your curse words enter their ears and are evaluated by their mind. Do you like your reason for cursing? Was it thoughtful, or have you given way to cursing because you are focused on yourself and how others perceive you?

A courteous curse has a few key components that I would encourage you to consider. Think of cursing as the last bit of your favorite makeup highlighter. This stuff is magnificent. Your cheeks are on point when you sweep on a little. It is perfect for those no-makeup days where you still want to work those face angles. You wake up one morning ready to conquer and slay and grab that precious bottle of highlighter only to realize that you have just a few sweeps left. You know you need to handle this precious bottle of amazing with care. Don't drop it. No over-sweeping. You need to dip that brush deliberately and place that highlighter ever so carefully. Too much highlighter, and you go from fab to daytime drag, which can be a look if you're deliberate. Too little highlighter, and it looks like you were afraid to go all in. It becomes a complete waste of precious makeup highlighter. This requires some deliberation because we are talking about your favorite expensive highlighter. It just got real.

Now think of cursing in much the same way. You want to use that same cautious deliberation. Too much, and you go from fab and funny to potty mouth real quick. Too little, and it sounds forced and awkward like you were trying too hard to squeeze in a curse word. You feel strange, and it's almost like you should leave cursing to the other grown-ups. Don't waste precious products by overuse in small amounts doled out blandly over time. There is no power, magic, or delight there. It is cursing for the sake of cursing, which is boring and rather useless. Deliberate placement is key, so too with cursing. A well-timed and well-placed curse word used with a deliberate sweep of speech is much more effective.

Conclusion

Your voice is one of your most valuable assets. What you say is as important as how you say it. To be fierce, feminine, and female does not require you to be a quiet, doormat, and the very last to speak. Instead, the requirement is that you consider the people you are talking to and be deliberate with your word choice. Nothing you say is worth beating yourself up over. Over-rumination does you a disservice.

Reflection and evaluation of what you said in the past is the best method for being deliberate going forward. Not to censor yourself, but because you understand that when you speak you can persuade and affect change. Your words carry power. Use them deliberately and, therefore, powerfully. Demonstrate your confidence in the words you are speaking and the thoughts you want to communicate by doing so deliberately. Word choice and delivery are key.

We don't need to use a laser blast power tool when a pair of tweezers will do the job, and vice versa. The best way to know which tool to use is to shut your glam hole and listen. Listen, and you will know whether to blast eloquently or bust out the big guns.

Now that more women are getting seats at the tables, let's make sure our seats are cemented by modeling for the women coming up behind us watching every move we make. You can leave a legacy of what not to do, or you can leave a legacy of confident, deliberate speech and mastery of the beauty in courteous conversation. Confident women leave legacies, and the way we speak is one way to achieve/create a legacy.

Think about our superhero with her cape and all of her super skills. Courteous conversation is one tool in her arsenal. It is a soft skill that she busts out during close quarter combat. She deploys this tool with super efficacy because she can watch her counterparts and separate fact from fiction in real-time. We've talked a lot about what not to do in this section and how to listen. In the next chapter, we will switch gears to taking stands and rising up. This was purposeful. Conversational courtesy first, how to take a stand next.

 **Homework**

Diagram three conversations you've recently had.

1. What the other person actually said
2. What you made it mean
3. What you actually said
4. What you think the other person made it mean

Do you notice the differences in each scenario, or the similarities?

What can you learn for the next conversation?

What will you do next time?

How do you want to feel next time you speak to this person?

What do you want to think next time you speak to this person?

Podcast Episode Guide

Episode 07: Other People's Opinions

Episode 31: Accepting Compliments

Episode 33: Self Confidence

Episode 62: Gift of Gab

Episode 72: Holiday Party Confidence

POISE AND DEPORTMENT:
How to Stand Up and Rise Up

Poise is about grace and elegance in being. Deportment describes your manners and behavior. So, poise and deportment is basically how to be and do. These words conjure up an elegant way of being and remind us of women marching in place with books on their heads or gliding gracefully into a chair without revealing their lady parts to the man seated across from them. (My mother refers to that as *taking a picture of someone*.) There are whole treatises on how to cross your ankles and not your legs. Most poise and deportment lessons in the past described how to hold your body in such a way as to be pleasing to the gaze of others, particularly the male gaze.

Today, we are less concerned with being the beautiful accessory at the table and more concerned with how to stand and rise as a fierce, feminine, female. We want to keep the lessons of poise and deportment and derive from those lessons the very best our mothers and grand-mothers had to offer us because there is value there. But now that we are standing in the room and commanding the presence of others, how do we want to stand up and rise in those situations? Now is your time, my darling. How do you want to show up? You have a choice.

Cape on, head high, heels on, lipstick check. Let's go!

Body Language: Going Old School and New School (Millennial issues with showing up)

Let's talk about body language. There are entire treatises and courses on body language, so I will limit our discussion to the three C's of body language and let you dive deep later if you want to do that. I am more concerned with you getting a basic understanding so you can engage in a quick application that is more useful to you. I will also share what I have learned as a coach and mentor for women who struggle with how they show up in the world and how other people perceive them.

Here is one thing I want to get through to you. Sometimes when enough people have an issue with how you speak and show up, the issue really is you and not that the world at large is out to get you. How you sit, stand, and speak sends signals. How you interpret the way others sit, stand, and speak interplays with your bodily responses. It becomes a feedback loop that requires you to master what your body is doing, what you are thinking, and what you do with your interpretation of the other people in the room.

Consider the three C's of body language, context, congruence, and clusters. [4] Context is just as it sounds. What the hell is going on around the person(s) speaking? Clusters require you to look at all the subtleties that lame court tv tell you will indicate the witness was lying: tone of voice, darting eyes, arm and hand placement, and if their face turns red or white. Congruence puts context and clusters together to determine whether the person speaking to you is credible.

I am not recommending you become an expert in reading body language. I am HIGHLY recommending you become aware of and develop expertise in your own body language. This brings us back to that awkward conversation with the person preoccupied with their own hands who gives off the creepy shifty vibe. They seem to have lost control of where their mind is wandering, and their ability to form coherent sentences and monitor what their body is doing. The pacing, beading sweat, wringing hands, and persistent face touching gives the picture of a nervous AF person. These seem rather obvious like this person has no mastery over what their body is doing.

---

[4] http://www.interviewexpertacademy.com/body-language-the-3c-triangle/

Let me give you a more subtle example. Do you rest your chin on your palm during meetings? Do you put your hands in your pockets when you speak in public? Do you stare at the mirror behind the person speaking to you? These are subtle examples of a lack of awareness and mastery over your body and body language. This is beyond elbows off the table during dinner, and has more import because a lack of self-awareness can cost you credibility and opportunity.

The goal is not to frighten you, but to raise your level of awareness. Being fierce, feminine, and female requires mastery over not only what you are wearing and what you say, but how you say it and how you are holding yourself when you say it. All of these things require some level of mastery. To reach mastery, we need to begin with awareness and then build your confidence.

The primary focus of old school education regarding poise and deportment was to modify behavior alone. The idea is that if you can master how to sit, stand, or walk gracefully, you can trick others into believing that you were a lady or well above your station. Then came the more updated version, body language, which is often presented as a sweet trick on legal shows, taught as lie-detecting trickery. Now, there is much ado about body language in interviews so that you do not appear closed off or unwelcoming. It seems to me that a lot of the emphasis is on behavior modification alone to appear more credible and attractive to others, as a job prospect or even a romantic prospect. Learning poise and deportment, or standing up like a freaking lady, should not be focused solely on attracting the male gaze or tricking people into believing you are trustworthy.

Thus, as in all things, my darling, we do both the mindset and the practical work. The mindset work informs our actions. Hereto, it is important to ensure that we are more concerned with what is going on in our own heads so we can change our actions from the inside out, as opposed to behavior modification alone, which feels fake and strange.

The idea is not to trick someone into believing that you are more confident than you feel, but to actually be confident and have that reflected in how you sit, walk, stand, and rise up.

Confidence: Capability, and Availability

Confidence and self-confidence are two subtly different concepts. Confidence is about capability; it is about the things you do. Self-confidence is all about availing yourself of that capability. Put another way: Confidence is about the things you do. Self-confidence allows you to do things.

A fashion model walks confidently down the catwalk because she has self-confidence. Confidence describes the things we do well, and it is tied to an external source of approval. Self-confidence is what allows us to do something, whether we do it well or not.

Models on the runway walk WITH confidence. However, sometimes they fall and trip. Their self-confidence allows them to get up and keep walking. They may not have walked well. They may be considered a failure. They may get up to a crowd booing or cheering. Self-confidence allows them to get up and keep going. It is not tied to their performance. Confidence describes the action. Self-confidence describes the person.

You may not be able to do things with confidence because you are out of practice or a newbie. Self-confidence is the inner capability to try despite skill or experience. If we needed to be experts before we can try anything, nothing would be accomplished or invented. This is such an important concept. Self-confidence will get you glammed up every day and dressed to the nines. You don't have to rely on external applause, special skills, or expertise. True self-confidence allows you to get up and strut (even when you sometimes fall in front of a crowd of a few hundred photographers).

That all sounds well and good, but I have discovered that the joy of missing out (JOMO) has often eroded any sense of self-confidence, even while it is budding. How can it erode even before it begins? Because women opt out of the event that would have allowed them to cultivate and strengthen their self-confidence.

For example, I had a client, Miss R, who had what she described as a very difficult client. Her client was rude, condescending, and demanding. There were endless emails from the rude client about how Miss R was brilliant and gifted at her chosen craft, but her delivery of information and bad news left a lot to be desired. For weeks, I worked with Miss R on crafting better-written communications. We discussed how to communicate via telephone so that each party could hear one another, confirm their understanding, and move on with a mutual understanding and plan of action. We were so close. So close.

Then came time to meet the client in person at a dinner party. There would be multiple clients in attendance, but this was really a chance for Miss R to get some face time and show up with the newfound confidence that we had been cultivating for weeks.

I will pause the story here. The confidence did not come because Miss R wrote better emails and shut her glam hole more often on phone calls. NO! The confidence developed because of a mindset shift that perhaps the issue was not the client. The self-awareness and self-responsibility kicked in. The willingness to decide to stop, listen, and approach things differently was an inside job that manifested outwardly.

Now, back to our story. Miss R had one mission: to approach the client, stand with the client at a cocktail table, and make small talk. Unfortunately, Miss R chose not to approach the client. She chose to stand back, even when her colleagues prompted her to approach the client. Miss R shrugged them off, then made the ultimate slap your forehead SMDH move. She bounced without so much as a "goodbye" or "how do you do?" Instead of braving what was likely to be uncomfortable for only a few moments is now cemented in a prolonged awkwardness because Miss R ghosted her client.

What does this have to do with body language and confidence? Everything. Nobody can ascertain your body language, meaning, or intentions if you no-show or ghost them. By opting out, you opt right out of the opportunity. You no-show, and there is nothing to redirect a miscommunication or clarify. The conversation then becomes one-sided, leaving the other person only to guess what you meant or what your intentions were. Everyone in this scenario is a grown-up and will have to manage their thoughts and feelings, but leaving another human alone with their imagination to decide what you meant by ghosting is not likely to result in a download of positive thoughts and feelings.

When you opt-out, no-show, or ghost, you are disrespecting the person you left hanging and taking a hatchet to your self-confidence. You are training your brain to opt-out of uncomfortable situations. It is like telling a toddler, "Oh, you don't want to go to the first day of preschool and play with the other kids? No problem, you don't have to." We would never allow a toddler to do that. We know that things will be sad and uncomfortable at first, other kids can be cruel (and that sometimes doesn't change as people age), BUT we do not let toddlers opt-out. When you allow yourself to be flakey and not show up, you are shooting your growth and learning potential in the foot.

Poor Miss R is a fictional character created from several people I know who had the habit of not showing up – to work, personal, and family events. They all got into the nasty habit of opting out of discomfort. They also lamented that they felt they had missed opportunities.

Confidence is about what you do at a modicum that requires you to actually show up. A model does not show up to a fashion show, she cannot walk down a runway with confidence. She never risks falling in front of reporters or photographers and being streamed on the internet in a highlight reel for all to see. However, she also misses the opportunity to nail it and be seen by other potential employers and brands. She also risks losing the opportunity to show what she is made of when she falls face first and has the self-confidence to get her booty back up and slay. She will miss out on the excellent future dinner party fodder of when she fell rocking Chanel in front of a few hundred international photographers.

You cannot develop confidence and self-confidence if you fail to appear. So, my darling, the most basic thing I can tell you is *show up*. Yes, it will be uncomfortable. You might sweat through your bra. You may say something totally stupid. We can work on those issues, but we can't undo or learn anything from you no-showing. To rise up and stand up like a boss, first requires you to show up.

Compare And Despair: Taking Up Space And Scanning A Room

Let's say you are brave enough to show up. You decide to enter the fray, the room, pony up at the table. How do you manage when all your brain wants to do is scan the room and compare you to the other people at the table? Scanning every room you enter to see how you measure up to the people around you will only leave you in despair. Compare and despair pretends to be necessary, but it isn't. You don't have to size up the room to feel confident. In fact, it is the perfect way to give your brain evidence that you should have stayed home. You must override your brain's tendency to categorize people and rank yourself in a hierarchy. (This is called heuristics.)

In my time as a coach and mentor, I have seen compare and despair show up in many ways. Scanning the room to see if: (1) you have the biggest body in the room, (2) you are the only female in the room, and/or (3) you are the only person of color in a room. Your brain will immediately scan the room to decide if you need to feel threatened or if there is someone with whom you share a common characteristic.

This is the old fight, flight, or freeze. Most people freeze and opt-out, or they show up only to desire to fight or flee. Use your prefrontal cortex to overcome the lower part of your brain convincing you to run away. Exercise that part of your brain, use your imagination, and decide on purpose ahead of time how you want to think, feel, and act before you enter the room. Deciding what to think in advance is the most crucial part of the "before you enter the room" rules that you can make.

What you are thinking about before you enter a room will inform how you feel and how you act once you are in the room. BUT you must consider ALL of this before you enter the room. The pre-game work matters the most. No, I am not talking about liquid courage from alcohol. I would advise against that. Don't lower your inhibitions when you are trying to create a deliberate in-the-room experience.

Deciding Ahead of Time

I learned the concept of making decisions ahead of time from my coach, Brooke Castillo[5]. I first applied this concept to create a protocol for my food choices. My decisions ahead of time were to help me stay conscious and overcome disordered eating patterns I had adopted through many diets. My decisions ahead of time were not to lose weight or perfectly master a diet. The concept was to create my food protocol myself by paying attention to my body, listening to its hunger signals, and being kind when my hunger signals got crossed with the desire to eat past full.

At its very heart, this concept is about having integrity with the commitments you make to yourself. Now, this sounds like behavioral modification again and not mindset work. Nope, I am here to tell you that deciding what you will or won't do ahead of time is all mental

---

[5] Master Certified Coach Instructor and Owner of the Life Coach School, Brooke Castillo

work. The decisions I made ahead of time years ago still serve me and carry me forward today. I still institute protocols around work and decide ahead of time what will get done and how much time I will allot to each task. My decisions ahead of time govern how I choose to spend or NOT spend my money. The guiding principle is always, "I will never beat myself up."

It sounds simple enough, but it is quite profound when practiced. To my overachieving ladies who are drilling "learn from your mistakes" in your head, stop. You are probably using that quote against yourself to justify over rumination about a perceived past mistake. When you decide ahead of time, you will no longer beat yourself up for any reason. Then, you can truly step back and observe what you would like to do differently, moving forward. That is a very different mindset than "learn from your mistakes," which has an underlying assumption that there was a mistake in the first place.

I would encourage you to make your first decision ahead of time be never to beat yourself up again, no matter what. That way, whenever you reflect on how you conducted yourself in a social setting, you can look with curiosity for real improvement rather than from a place of judgment.

Deciding What to Think

Let's talk about what to think about before you enter the room (work meetings, conferences, social gatherings, etc.). There is no perfect or right thought here. It really will come down to how the different thoughts feel when you try them on. The time you will likely spend deliberating how to think and what to think before entering the meeting is similar to the effort you put into selecting a suit or blouse for a meeting. Think of how amazing or scary a prospect that is, depending on how much time you dedicate to how you dress yourself.

Think of thoughts like outfits you are going to try on until you find the right fit for you. Every fabulous jacket needs tailoring, that is what gives it its fabulousness. You will also tailor your thoughts by checking in with yourself. When the fit is right, it feels right and you immediately find yourself standing taller swinging from side to side, admiring yourself. We call this preening. The same is true with a useful thought.

Thoughts to practice before entering a room have to do with how you want to show up when entering the room. Do you want to show up as a total lady boss and a problem-solving mediator? Do you need to ensure that you communicate your ideas to a team of people? Are you trying to be persuasive? Every situation will differ. So, how do you know? You practice some old-school junior sleuthing techniques.

First, consider how the invitation to this meeting or gathering came to you. Was it a formal work memo? Was the invitation printed on formal stationery? Was this a quick email or text message to get your booty to x place at y time. The *how* of the invitation will give you some clues about how you decide to present yourself in the situation. Formality in the invite will inform formality in attendance. Remember the three C's of body language. Context is King. The method in which the invitation was delivered to you provides context to how you should show up to the occasion.

Second, consider what time of day you are meeting. Again, more context clues for how you should approach and show up to the situation. Evening usually begets less formality, but not always. Quick brunch even less formality, but not always. During work hours or close to the end of the day will also provide you clues about the nature of the situation.

Third, consider who will be present. Now, I know it is super millennial to ask, "Who is going to be there?" This is a not a catty way to fish as to whether someone is worth your time. Let's assume we are required to attend or have already decided ahead of time not to ignore invitations and to show up to places we have committed to showing up. In which case, knowing *who* is going to be there will allow you to create your conversation plan and be prepared to talk to others at the meeting

Fourth, decide ahead of time *what* you will say. No, I am not suggesting you create a creepy script of every laugh and gesture you will make. Young attorneys tend to do that at trial when questioning witnesses. Then, they become frustrated when the witness doesn't answer as they expected, and it throws them off of their script. The *what* of social interaction takes the contextual clues you've been given (where, when, and how) so you can create a conversation plan and won't end up standing in the corner like a wallflower waiting for conversation to come to you. It gives your brain focus when it may get giddy at the thought of conversing with a difficult client or people you have never met. Here is your chance to formulate some questions that don't center on "What do you do?" Instead, you can prepare more meaningful questions like, "Working on anything exciting lately?" The latter is a better question because it invites conversation and narrative. "What do you do," invites a one-word answer and an awkward pause.

A conversation plan considers the contextual clues and gives you some places to start with what to say. Pause for a moment and think about how refreshing and confidence-inducing it will be when your brain tries to convince you not to show up, and you remind it that you already have a plan in place. You have decided to show up, to talk to at least one person, to graciously thank your host for the invite, and to adopt the conversation starter you have already decided to lead with. Think of how this game plan affects your confidence level. If you are naturally extroverted and enjoy gabbing, I would still encourage you to think of conversation starters that are open-ended and invite narrative rather than closed-ended questions. This will ensure the focus is on the person with whom you are speaking rather than yourself.

When we go in to a situation with thoughts like "I have a plan" or "I've got this," it affects our mood. Our mood will affect our body language. You are not a mind operating without a body. You need all parts cued in, and the best way to achieve that is to engage your brain first so it can inform your mood and your body language second.

Deciding What to Feel

Now that we've used contextual clues to inform what you will think before you enter the situation, we will use those decisions ahead of time to inform how you want to feel when you enter the room. There is an interplay amongst each of these, and the best way to know if a thought decided on ahead of time will produce the confidence you want is to test it and check in with yourself.

For example, telling yourself things like, "You should be charming and know what to say. You've done this a million times," may sound like a bit of an innocuous pep talk, but it can actually be quite insipid if it makes you feel like crap when you think that thought. The goal isn't to use the work against yourself, beat yourself into submission, and drag yourself into situations where you truly feel uncomfortable. That most certainly will be evident in your body language when you show up.

The principle here is that you get to decide how you want to feel before you walk into any room. You choose how you want to feel once you are in a room, no matter what is happening. You get a choice. So, think about what feeling you want to cultivate beforehand. This is not a *fake it until you make it* thing revamped. Your body language will show how you really feel, no matter how many mantras you scream at yourself before an event. Don't let your body language betray you. Get in sync with it by checking in with how you feel when you decide ahead of time how you want to feel. Here is how you can check in with yourself to know if your conversation and thought plan will work for you.

Acknowledge The Actual Thought You Are Having Now

So many of my clients learn that they can choose what they think and how they feel, so they want to jump to a new more positive thought immediately. The problem is that you are lying to yourself. It is akin to trying to convince your brain that the sun is shining and the sky is blue during a rainstorm. You can tell yourself in a chirpy sounding mantra that the sky is blue and the sun is shining all you want, but the rainfall does not give a damn about your chirpy mantra. The goal isn't to wish things other than they are by telling yourself nice-sounding platitudes that you do not believe.

Nay, the goal is to acknowledge and accept where you currently are so you can address whatever concerns come up. For example, admitting that it is raining before you step out of the house to walk to work is of more use than pretending that it's not raining. Instead, acknowledge that it's raining and prepare yourself accordingly with rain boots, rain coats, and umbrellas. It shouldn't be a surprise to you that your "Rain, rain, go away" mantra didn't work.

If you have an upcoming meeting with your boss, a client happy hour, or some other social gathering, and you are starting to feel anxious, before telling yourself over and over that "you're a boss," acknowledge that you may not feel like one at this particular moment. Instead, you are thinking thoughts like "Holy crap, why is this meeting happening? I'm in trouble. I must've screwed something up..." Be honest with yourself about what is going on up there so you can prepare your brain with your analogous version of boots, raincoats, and umbrellas. For example, you can always ask yourself why the meeting is happening, and review your recent work projects to see if there was a real screw up or an imaginary ever-present one.

I used to have scary "imaginares," which occur when my imagination quickly converts everything into a nightmare. When I was younger, I was absolutely convinced that scary things lived under my bed and would grab my hand or leg if they dangled off the side of the bed. It would get so bad that I would wake up my sister, Cheli, with whom I shared a room. I would tell her to roll to one side of her bed so I could leap from my bed to hers without touching the floor. The floor was lava and monsters. I also feared that gremlins lived in the toilet and would flush and run every single time, causing me to run face-first into a closed doorway several times.

The problem is, as adults, we still do this with our thoughts. The "monster" under our childhood bed was just a pile of socks or a deviously-placed Lego waiting to impale itself in the bottom of your foot. There were no monsters. If we don't stop to acknowledge our thoughts, then we still have this nagging doubt in the back of our brain that the pile of socks was indeed a monster. Nope, instead, you have to get on the floor, lift the covers, look under the bed, feel around, pull out the socks, blow the dust bunnies off, and throw them in the hamper.

Your brain requires the same acknowledgment. Pull out the thoughts, blow the dust off of them, lift up all of the assumptions you have stacked upon that thought, and decide where to place that thought – "useful" or "unuseful." For example, I always used to think "I'm in trouble." Even when I got a promotion, I asked my boss if I was in trouble. He laughed then looked at me as if he was both puzzled and worried. Why on earth would I think that thought? Habit. I was unaware of this particular sock monster until it was pointed out by my dear coaching friends who called me out on this thought.

We sat on the proverbial floor and pulled that sock thought out from under the bed. How long had that been there? Since I was a little kid. Was it useful? No. Did I want to keep thinking that? Not particularly. Was I magically cured of this old dusty sock thought? Nope, but each time I heard myself ask that question in my head or heard it pop out of my mouth, I recognized it for what it was. An old sock thought.

Think about old sock thoughts you have roaming around in your brain. I challenge you to write them down. That is how you pull them out from under the bed into the light so you can see them objectively. Next, dust that sucker off. How long has it been there? Is it useful to you? Do you want to continue to think that thought? Do this before you ever consider replacing the old sock thought with a new one.

How Does It Feel?

How do we know if we think a sock is a monster? Easy, how do you feel when you think about what is under your bed? Your thoughts produce an emotion. The sock was always a sock, but it became a monster when we had some thoughts about it. Those thoughts cause us to feel fear. We can attempt to rationalize with ourselves, as we do with toddlers, that there is nothing there. We can assure ourselves it is no big deal. We can go through the motions of checking and double-checking, but if we still believe there is a monster and not a sock, then that fear remains. That is how we know whether a new thought is something we truly believe or something we are merely trying on for size. We check in with how we are feeling.

Let's take it back to our client cocktail party. If you are afraid of meeting the client in person because you think they already hate you, you got off to a bad start, or you dislike the client for requiring you to undergo communications coaching for the last few weeks, your emotions will reflect all of those thoughts. The fear, anxiety, and hatred are all there because of the thoughts you're thinking. Let's say you try to cover up that thought with a, "It will be okay" or, "It's not that big a deal." Do you really believe that? Probably not, especially if you are still feeling that fear, anxiety, and hatred. You can tell yourself those things all you want, but if you don't believe it, your body will send a signal to your brain that you are still afraid, anxious, or hateful.

How do you go from not believing to believing? You start small and build up, similar to the body image work from previous chapters.

Add these pre-thought belief sequences to the thoughts you want to believe and check in with your body along the way. For example, "It is possible that it will be okay." If you cannot believe that and don't get any relief from your anxiety, add another pre-thought sequence. "It is possible that other people think this is not a big deal?" If your brain is sarcastic like mine, it may tell you that other people can suck it. Then I try on for size, "It is possible that maybe one day this will not be a big deal." Each time I add a pre-thought sequence, I check in with myself. Am I feeling some relief? Does the anxiety, fear, or doubt subside?

Again, just like we don't want to jump to a new chirpy thought immediately, our goal is not to always run around feeling happy. There is nothing wrong with feeling some amount of fear or anxiety. These tell us when there is real danger. Our brains are wired to keep us safe from famine, lions, and pestilence. We want those cues to real danger to be firmly intact. We don't want to override them with feigned happiness continually. However, when we look at our thoughts and feelings objectively, it helps to step back and see if there really is a danger of famine, lions, or pestilence. Likely not for most of you reading this book. That may not be true of someone living in conditions where that is not a regular occurrence. I cannot speak to the dangers they face daily, while I do acknowledge them. However, I can tell you about the perceived dangers of working in a white-collar workplace where you feel that your boss is very much a lion. But, he is *not* a lion, and you are *not* prey.

It is imperative you understand this. Your brain will perceive dangers to be real and ever-present. Your job is to remind it what a healthy amount of anxiety and fear is given the actual circumstances presented to you. Remember, you are walking into an air-conditioned room, with nice-ish furniture, surrounded by other humans who all poop. You will exchange words, and at this time tomorrow, you will be home chillin. A month from now, this may be such a distant memory that you will have to go out of your way to remind yourself this meeting ever took place. Really think about that. Getting eaten by a lion is memorable, but walking into an air-conditioned room with other humans exchanging sounds and then leaving is not the same level of danger. Keep that in mind, my friend.

A sock is not a monster until we think it is one. The ability to go from the woman who opts out and no-shows to the one who shows up fabulous, feminine, and fierce is confidence. Confidence is availing yourself of your capability. You can only do that if you show up and face the fear. You have to crawl under the bed and pull out the sock. You have to show up to the cocktail hour and stand in front of the client. You've got this, boo. Getting from the no-show to the triple F is learning to dial in to how you want to feel, and practicing that until it becomes real.

Think About How You Want to Feel

As humans, we have the magical ability to not only think about our thoughts but also to put language around our feelings. We have sensations in our body that we call shame, anxiety, fear, worry, doubt, joy, happiness. No other species on this planet can put language around a sensation in their body or a chemical cascade that has happened in a particular pattern from our brain to our hormones to our muscles that we then recognize as dread. Stop for a second and think about how absolutely mind bendy and amazing that is. We are marvelously made creatures.

This magical ability to put language to a sensation in your body and to attribute it to a certain emotion has a twofold magical quality. One, you can name what you are currently feeling, which we discussed at length above. Two, you can choose what you want to feel and reverse the chemical process from your prefrontal cortex to your hormones and your muscles, as opposed to the involuntary manner in which emotions seem to appear, move through, and then show up as a different emotion from one moment to the next. This may sound woo AF, but it really isn't, and the purpose of this book is not to give you a scientific treatise on the way that it works. You gotta trust Miss J that this is true or be a diligent lady boss and research it all on your own. (Which I highly recommend you do, boo-boo.) For our purposes, I am giving you the basic overview of some life-changing *ish* so you can conquer and model it for the other women. How does one woman appear to be serene when the world seems to swirl in chaos around her? She may be putting on a brave face, or we can give credit where credit is due and acknowledge that woman put in work to show up like a boss in the face of adversity.

So, my darling, I want to teach you this same meta-skill. After you look at your thoughts objectively and name the current feelings that arise in you, dust that thought off and evaluate both. Notice that sense of relief that buoys up inside you. Then, shift focus to what you want to feel.

My go-to emotions are not necessarily happiness or confidence. My favorite go-to emotions are to feel resolved, deliberate, wise, and masterful. These are much more useful to me in everyday life. Confidence is a great start; it means you have shown up and put your hat in the ring even when you acknowledged that there was some residual doubt or worry. You still showed up to avail yourself of your capability.

Now, when you start to do that on the regular, you get to a point where you need a little more oomph to keep that mojo going. For me, the next tier was to focus on feeling resolved. Why resolved? I chose that particular emotion because it evokes a steadfast, unwavering fortitude to stick to a decision I made ahead of time. Now, this isn't blind adherence out of stubbornness – that has an entirely different sensation than resolve. However, they are close cousins, and the only way I will know if I have crossed over from resolve to stubborn is by being completely honest with the thought behind the emotion. "Because I said so," may sound boss but can also be just straight-up stupid stubbornness. You really will know the nuanced differences.

Let's think about our cocktail hour with Miss R. What emotion would serve her well in that scenario? What outcome is she trying to achieve? How has she already decided in her mind that she wants to show up? What kind of a woman does she want to be when she enters the room, stands in the room, and leaves the room? She gets to decide every single step of the way. Remember, we have the beautiful ability to put language to what we are feeling, and, therefore, choose ahead of time how we want to feel.

Yes, there will be an ebb and flow to the emotion you choose. It may feel strong, then taper and waver. We have discovered that emotions move through us, so if you get a heart twinge or flutter of anxiety, remember it will move through you and pass. Then, redirect your brain to the emotion you chose ahead of time. This is useful in a negotiation. You leave room for give-and-take, but if you choose to be resolved, wise, and/or savvy, think about how you will pull your chair up to that table instead of feeling insecure, doubtful, or worried. Acknowledge that those feelings come up, allow them to move through, and redirect. It is more art than science and requires practice, practice, practice.

From the thought to your feeling, these will ultimately determine how you behave in any given social situation. The first thought is to decide to show up and not beat yourself up. no matter what occurs. Then, choose how you want to think and feel. Now it is time to spring into action. Thinking and feeling will determine how you show up and how you behave. Each step of the way remember that you choose how you show up in the world. Once you decide to show up like a boss and fully own that boss lady persona, then your actions will mirror those decisions ahead of time. That is not to say everything will go smoothly or according to plan, but I discourage you from playing out imaginary scripted conversations in your head. Determine to show up and to show up confidently. This will allow you to be present enough to respond meaningfully, no script required. We are not over-thinking; we are choosing what to think on purpose. There is a difference.

Last, remember the triple F threat: female, feminine, and fierce. Confident women leave legacies. The woman who shows up is more apt to grow and model for other women what it means to show up, and then show up again even when you fail. She has more to teach and to grow than the woman who decides not to show up at all. In our fashion show example, the model who gets up on the runway and continues to saunter after she falls is more likely to be called the conquering hero or the brave one than the woman who crawls backstage never to be seen or heard from again. Self-confidence requires some falling down; getting back up is what matters the most.

You are 100% worthy and 100% capable. Will you avail yourself of both? What is the worst that can happen? You may feel embarrassed. Remember, that hormone cascade only lasts a moment in your body before you are onto another emotion. You will only perpetuate embarrassment with the thoughts you think. So, decide now and commit now that you will show up, and no matter what happens, you will no longer beat yourself up. You will get up, even when you fall, and saunter on.

**Homework**

Think this through...You have an upcoming event:

1. How did the invitation come to you?
2. Who sent it?
3. What time is the event/meeting/situation/gathering?
4. What are you thinking about it right now?
5. What are you feeling about it right now?
6. How do you want to feel?
7. What do you want to think?

Give me at least three decisions ahead of time that you are making for this event?

For example: I will show up. I will not beat myself up afterward no matter what happens.

Podcast Episode Guide

Episode 33: Self Confidence

Episode 62: Gift of Gab

Episode 72: Holiday Party Confidence

Episode 71: How to Find a Holiday Party Dress

GUMPTION: Because You Are Not Just Another Pretty Face

Gumption Then and Now

When you hear words like gumption and pluck, your brain may automatically think of an old black and white film with funny slang like "waxing moxy" and the beautiful sidekick, or the girl Friday who advances the schemes of the main character. She can also be the pretty side piece or the nefarious cheating wife of the poor, misunderstood fella. You could be cast as a leading ladies, but often those roles came at a high cost: the man you love, propriety, modesty, and/or femininity. You couldn't be a beautiful, fierce, and feminine leading lady.

I think specifically of the movie *Philadelphia Story* with Katherine Hepburn. She was beautiful and fierce, but my goodness, all of the comments about her being cold and unfeeling... it is as though her beautiful ferocity made her femininity mutually exclusive. Her character was referred to as a statute and a block of ice. Eventually, she comes around, but only after jilting her fiancé and making out with James Stewart before returning to her husband, Dexter, played by Carey Grant. Again, to be all three had its price.

The underlying message of the old version of gumption was that a woman cannot have it all without paying a price. It was almost dangerous to have brains and beauty at the same time. The movies presented to us the untold dangers of spinsterhood and loneliness. There are some things to love and admire about the old version of gumption, but we need women to fully own the role of leading lady. To step into the character who moves the plot forward with her actions and has the gumption to dream and dream big. The role of a lifetime is waiting for you, my darling. Are you ready?

Why Does Gumption Matter?

Gumption means to show initiative, determination, and courage. To be the woman who writes her own story and advances the plot forward requires all three. In this chapter, we will discuss goal setting while using all of the lady gumption you've got. It requires initiative, determination, and courage. Of most import, it requires you to show up as your entire self: fierce, feminine, and female.

Gumption matters because it requires more than an amazing idea that you write in that pretty journal you purchased and forgot about. It requires you to keep going until you achieve what you set out to achieve. Gumption requires more than being brave on one particular occasion. It is a feeling and an attribute. It is something you cultivate through hardship and failure. I know that sounds pretty damn awful when I put it like that, but it really is the skill required to achieve your dreams and turn hopes into reality. Anyone can dream, and even crazy drunk people have courage, but gumption requires you to cultivate all three attributes. The woman with gumption is the leading lady. She is something altogether different. She has a Mae West attitude, Katherine Hepburn wit, and Rosalind Russell can do.

The woman without gumption never gets past the pretty idea in the notebook. She gives up after the first failure or fails to launch at all. Without gumption, it is hard to keep going when the naysayers come out of the woodwork, even the well-intended ones. The woman with gumption is sold on hard work because she is determined to see what she is made of when she adds fire and pressure to her own life on purpose. Yes, she can be the supporting actor, but the leading ladies have all of the fun. Yes, all eyes may feel like they are on you. Maybe you will be required to take on a bigger role and stand out in a crowd. You are 100% capable. With even just a smidgen of gumption, who knows what you will create.

It Was All A Dream

If you saw that line and immediately started rapping "Juicy," I seriously love you. If you have no idea what I am talking about, Google it. When my maternal grandparents, who were both Puerto Rican, were in their thirties, they lived in New York, and owned a Double-A baseball team called the Hatillo Tigers. I cannot impress upon you enough how big a deal baseball is with my family.

My grandparents were not wealthy. My grandpa dropped out of elementary school. My grandmother, the brains, was a woman of color during the 60s in New York with a Puerto Rican accent. These two didn't know any better than to dream big and to do it up big. So, they bought a baseball team. I don't know the whole story. I know that there are some amazing pictures of my grandmother in a blue dress when the team won a championship. I also know there are pictures of my grandmother with some pretty women wearing the team colors. The family never talks about how the baseball team was lost or sold. Nope, the story that gets passed down is that my grandpa loved baseball and they bought a baseball team.

Here's the thing, whenever you tell your future stories of success or loss, you decide the parts of the story you tell. I wasn't able to give you much information because frankly, I don't have very much to give. I know my grandparents had a dream, they fulfilled that dream, and the story ends there because the original storyteller didn't think it was that important. It started as a dream, and it became a reality. Now, I could tell that differently. It was all a dream until it wasn't, and they lost the baseball team they worked so hard to obtain. That would be putting dubs on it, but you get the point. I can also tell you a heroic tale of two crazy immigrant kids from different sides of the track, one beauty and the other the brains, a true New York Tale, and they fulfilled their lifelong dream of owning a baseball team. Every Puerto Rican kid's dream come true. A real American New York story. I could tell you that version, too.

Too often, we never even get started on our dreams because we get caught up in how we will narrate the eventual story. Was it a failure? Was it a success? How will I tell my parents, my boyfriend, my so-and-so? Everyone else becomes the lead in our story, except us. We stop driving the plot ourselves, and we look to everyone else's reactions to determine how we tell our story and how we evaluate whether our dream came true. Leading ladies with gumption leave the storytelling for the other people; they merely come to work. They don't factor so-and-so into the life they are leading or the eventual story they are going to tell.

My darling, before we get started making your dreams into a reality, remember that you get to write a tale of woe or a real-life American rags to riches New York story. For now, leave the story writing to others. You go live a great, large life, and the story will write itself.

How to Cultivate Gumption

Initiative

Initiative is two-fold: dreaming and planning. Anyone can dream big and tell you all about one day how they might do such and such thing. The lady with gumption dreams and PLANS how she will achieve her dreams. Her plans are not just an exercise in pretty journaling with gel pens. Nope, she has mastered breaking down her big giant dreams into tiny bit-size steps that she can put on a calendar and generate wins for herself. She doesn't talk about what she will create *someday*; she will tell you what she is doing *today* to make that *someday* a reality. Initiative requires action. It cannot just happen in your head, or you will never make it past the dreaming phase.

Let's begin with the concept of dreaming. Some of the women I have coached were stuck at this phase because they have stopped dreaming, or they censor their dreams before writing the idea in a journal. You cannot plan what you do not allow to fully birth from your heart to your head then to your pen. This is your permission, in case you needed it, to dream big, and to do so without censoring yourself. Dream big without telling yourself why it will never work and then dismissing yourself prematurely.

Your first homework assignment in the Gumption chapter is to dream big giant New York sized dreams. Write down everything you have ever wanted to create, see, do, or experience. All of it. I MEAN ALL OF IT. No matter how big or small. No matter how seemingly silly or insignificant. Do not censor yourself. Really allow yourself the opportunity to free-write.

If it has been a really long time since you allowed yourself an impractical brainstorming session, there is no time like the present to get back into that habit of writing all of the things that your heart desires with unadulterated bliss.

When I was younger, my grandmother and I would play accountant. It sounds like a strange game to play with a little kid, but my grandmother was not a kid person. She wasn't warm and fuzzy, but she had her way of relating to us that makes me appreciate her more and more the older I become. Our game of accountant would begin like this. She had a large collection of sad clown figurines (I am not sure what to make of this collection other than I will never fully understand the woman my grandmother was, and I have a lot of questions to ask her when I get to heaven.) We were not allowed to touch her sad clowns other than to help her dust them. This was part of the game. She would cut up old t-shirts into rags that we could use to dust her clowns carefully. She had a meticulous nature and would watch me while I dusted. Never criticizing, but always giving feedback along the way.

After I finished dusting, she would pull a 3x5 card from a gray box stored inside her large tanker desk. In beautiful penmanship, my name was written at the top. Each time I would dust, she would record my earnings on the 3x5 card . She taught me about balancing books and how to be responsible with the money I earned. I could make with-drawals, but that would be reflected on the notecard so I had to really think hard about it. I also had to consider whether it was worth my time to continue dusting for what I was earning. Of most import, she imparted to me the idea that you could write down the things you wanted and check to see if you had saved enough to purchase said items. In case you haven't noticed, my grandma was a freakin genius. Playing accountant isn't the stuff of Hallmark movies. But she in-stilled in me very early on the idea that you could write down what you wanted, check to see if you have what you needed to obtain what you wanted, and decide whether it was worthwhile to you to continue or change course. It was objective and it was about numbers. There was no drama infused in to this game.

When I was old enough to make Christmas lists, I wrote them in columns and rows. What I wanted, where it could be purchased, and approximately how much it would cost. My mother could then decide if she had sufficient means to obtain the items listed. I did this while also still firmly believing in Santa Claus. I was a practical dreamer then, and I still am.

So let's take the lesson of my Grandma Leida and play accountant on a larger scale. Dream big and write down all of the things that you want. I don't want you to consider whether you have the means or the ability to obtain what you want. The first goal is to document all of your wants. After you have written down absolutely everything that you dream of, think in terms of time periods. What would you like to achieve over a lifetime? 10 years from now? Five years from now? Three years from now? Within the next year? If it came down to just one item from that list of amazing ideas, which would you choose to create within the next year? Pick one. And lesgo!

Now, really assess your current situation. What do you need to know, do, or learn to obtain your dream? Write down absolutely every single step that you can think of based on your current knowledge base. If there is something you need to learn, then write that down. If there is a person you need to speak to, write that down. Even something as silly sounding as Googling information about who to talk to so you can learn something, that gets written down too. Show your brain that it is not a matter of impossibility, but sometimes a matter of accumulating some additional know-how, which is most definitely within your range of capability. You may not understand now, but you most certainly can learn. Don't shut yourself down at the dreaming stage because you don't know something yet.

Determination and Massive Action

Once you determine the one thing you want to create within the next year, it is time to get specific. I have a client who kept telling me she wanted to make a million dollars. When I asked her how she planned to make her first three thousand dollars, she melted into tears. Notice when the dream seemed larger than life, and very far away, there was no drama because a part of her brain believed it was impossible, so there was no reason to fret about it. Turn that dream into something smaller, specific, and tangible, then in comes the drama. Now, I am not criticizing her. I had the same issue when I first started in business. I would make big pronouncements about what I envisioned for the future and what I wanted to create. It sounded so beautiful and lovely, but also very vague, ensuring that I would never get near achieving that goal. Because I wasn't specific, even when I had some success, I would move the target, and the current win was ensured never to be "good enough." Eventually, I caught onto my brain and ended this cycle by turning vague, lofty notions into a very specific and concrete goal. Yes, let's make your business or any endeavor you might have a success, but stop and be specific about what we are working towards so we will know when we have arrived. A million dollars sounds good. Making your first $3,000 in the next three months is where the dreamers step into reality.

This is where the second part of gumption comes in. Gumption requires determination past the dreaming phase and planning phases. Let's say you make your one big dream specific. You want to make a million dollars over the next three years and are committed to making your first three thousand in the next three months. You are riding that initial dopamine high. The pretty plan you've created in your pretty journal is ready to be taken to the masses. Then nothing happens. Your three-month deadline is quickly approaching. You've a month to go, and nothing has happened yet.

The lady with gumption keeps showing up. She takes massive action fueled by the feeling of determination. She thinks, "I will keep going until I achieve the result I set out to achieve." She racks up failures as though they were wins. She stands on them and looks out over the kingdom she is building. When something doesn't work, she stands on top of that massive pile of failures and uses it as the foundation for the success she is building. That doesn't mean she continues to do things that clearly are not working, but she also does not quit altogether because 1,000 people didn't "Like" her social media post the first day she created her account. Massive action requires the lady with gumption to keep going, trying new things, or old things in new combinations. She won't know what worked until it does. She won't know something worked until she is sure that she has reached that original, very specific goal. She keeps on keepin on because she is determined to take action until she gets the result she set out to achieve.

This means showing up even when you don't feel like it. And there will be days where you definitely don't feel like it. Massive action means doing the hard stuff first. There will be a lot of delayed gratification and saying no to the things that don't matter so you can make room and time in your head and your heart for the things that do matter. You will need to be able to tune out the external voices of well-meaning friends and family members.

Whatever is happening and whoever is doing the talking, keep taking action.

Courage

The last part of the gumption trio is courage. Determination is the feeling driving you taking massive action until you get the result you desire. Courage is the feeling that drives you to keep your mindset in focus, which is required until you get the result you desire. Think of determination as massive action and courage as massive thinking. You will need both to get the result you want to achieve.

Massive thinking is a concept I learned from one of my teachers, Kara Lowentheil[6], that means practicing a thought until it becomes a reality. Let's look back at our million-dollar goal. It is hard to earn a million dollars when you are taking no action. You ensure that it will remain impossible when you think that it is impossible, and repeat that thought to yourself over and over again. So, we scale back the thought like we scale back our goal. We take it to the $3,000 level. You practice the thought, "I will make $3,000," and then, "I can make $3,000" until you have taken enough action so that the thought practiced becomes your new reality, "I have made $3,000." Then you scale it up again and again.

Doubt will creep in, my darling. Worry will show up because it always pretends to be necessary when you are doing something uncomfortable. All of your insecurity will rise to the surface. It is supposed to. Keep taking action until you get your result. Practice the thought until you get your result. When doubt, worry, and fear inevitably surface, you must create a process for dealing with these little thought burglars. Answer them with a strategy.

---

[6] Master Certified Life Coach and Creator of the Unfck Your Brain Podcast, Kara Lowentheill

Every doubt, worry, and fear is nothing but a thought obstacle. It is trying to stand in your way. You can quit and curl up at the bottom of this barricade, or you can answer that obstacle with a strategy. Toddlers experience this when they are learning to walk. Often they curl up in a heap because the truck is in their way, but they learn quickly they can push the truck to the side, step over it, or crawl right on over it. Crisis averted, obstacles past.

Adults forget they have this ability. We can strategize a way through our perceived problems, around it, or over it. Yeah, we may occasionally end up in a giant heap on the floor, then we let our rational brain kick in, and we strategize. Start to use that massive thinking. What would the woman who has achieved what I want do? What did she do? What did she think? How did she feel?

Stop and write a letter to yourself from that future place. Realize how much freaking common sense you have stored in that brain of yours when you move out of your own damn way because the reality is you are your worst enemy. Your thoughts are the only obstacle. Step away, regroup, and of most import, RETHINK.

But what about actual enemies? Naysayers? Frenemies? The toxic people who are holding you back from everything you ever wanted or desire? What about them? (Psst...they don't exist. There are no toxic people.)

The Should Committee, Villains, and Frenemies

We talk about being a lady boss, but we also talk about bad energies and toxic people in the same brain. A human literally cannot be toxic in the same way that arsenic is literally toxic. Another human has no power to prevent you from doing anything (absent being enslaved and held against your will – yes, that does exist). Having people around you or uttering noise in your direction is not toxic to your health, mental or otherwise.

The reality is that you already think insecure thoughts about yourself which are there because that is part of the human experience. It doesn't make you less enlightened or in need of realignment. It means you occasionally have thoughts that make you feel crappy. Welcome, fellow human. Other humans utter and grunt noises in your direction, and your brain interprets whatever that noise was to confirm your already present fears, worries, or doubts. If you truly don't have any of the above, no matter what noise is uttered in your direction, it won't matter. You don't need to make dramatic pronouncements on social media about how you are done, it's over, you are cutting out the toxic people, or any other passive aggressive meme that states it is for nobody in particular, but you secretly meant it for a few dozen people you have deemed toxic.

Consider that when you declare other people toxic and judge their behavior followed up with a "no judgment" disclaimer, you are exhibiting the very behavior you are judging. Perhaps you are the toxic one.

You are using the utters and grunts of others to prove your negative thoughts about you true. If you really thought you were a lady boss, you could see the utters and grunts as they really are, just noise you can take in or ignore.

Think about when you are in a noisy restaurant. You have to work hard to distinguish the voice of the person speaking directly to you from those voices around you. Your brain has to work to silence the background noise and focus on the person in front of it. It is remarkable that the brain can do this since the ambient noise level doesn't decrease. Your brain can filter what it wants when it desires and filter out noise that it finds unhelpful. The question is not one of toxicity or agreement with another person's noise thrown in your direction; the question is whether it is useful to filter out all of the other voices and focus on the one person. You always have a choice. Usually, the voice we focus on to distinguish from the others is the one that agrees with our own negative bias about ourselves.

Pay attention when you put too much emphasis on one person's opinion above all others. Why this particular person? When they give their opinion, what do you make it mean about you? Do you equate their opinion with arrival? Approval? Success? Worth? You are making their words mean something about you. You may perceive it as good and criticism as negative. I've also had clients who felt the inverse. They respected criticism and felt revulsion when praised. Neither is inherently negative; it all comes down to what you make it mean about you. Check in with yourself when you find yourself fixated on the opinions of an individual or group.

What About When You Know You Should Have Done Something Better Or Differently?

Oh, the lovely "should committee" – the group of critics in your head that are quick to point out "what you should've done was…" I had the "should committee" playing in my head for years. No matter what I did, it was never good enough. I could always have done it better or should have done it differently. There was always some version of could, should, would, and I felt exhausted and defeated until I learned a short, powerful question. "Says who?"

It took me a while to dismantle and sift through all of the people I believed were telling me what I should, could, and would do differently or better. Then I asked, "Well, when did *they* say that?" For the most part, nobody had told me how to conduct myself in a very long time. Not since I was a child, actually. So, "*Who* said?" Well, me. It was all me and only me every single day.

It was both freeing and worrisome. There was no actual external committee meeting to criticize my every decision or action. It was just little old me convening a committee every day to discuss everything I said or did. It was just me, which meant that I could decide to adjourn the committee meeting. I had the ability to turn off the committee or listen to their suggestions, choose to accept or deny them, and then move it along. When you hear that voice coming at you with the should, could, or would have, step back and remember that the only voice happening up there is YOUR voice. It is a committee of one. Those are your opinions, worries, doubts, and fear. That truly is good news because we have no control over what other people say, do, think, or feel. But we do have control over what we say, do, think, and feel. The best clap back is the one that happens in your head and empowers you to keep rolling with your plans.

What About Other People's Opinions?

Many high-achieving women I know use feedback and praise as the motivator for everything they do. They believe it has fueled them to get as far as they have, and not heeding the advice or opinion of someone whom they admire will doom them to failure. My brain operated this way for a really long time. I fully acknowledged all that my family and done for me and the foundation they laid for me to get as far as I have. I acknowledge it, and I am grateful for it. However, there came a time where gratefulness turned to a strange pattern of being beholden to their opinions and praise before I felt I could take up an endeavor. This was no fault of theirs. It was all mine because I believed for so long that I was fueled by their praise.

There were so many pictures taken of me when I was younger standing on top of a table or striking a pose and hamming it up. I used to enlist my poor sister Jessica in all of my shenanigans. One of my favorite pictures of us is from when we were ages three and four, and we are standing on top of the coffee table in our living room with Halloween buckets on our heads putting on a show. I was always producing shows. Even in high school, what was originally a simple fashion show hosted by Macy's turned into an all-out choreographed extravaganza with hosts and crazy mean girl-fueled popularity contests. (I was already running things like a boss then.) Front row every time, Jessica. Staying late to hang out with me for the endless rehearsals, Jessica. My personal hype crew.

I had a hard time in college because my hype crew wasn't there with me. I adjusted, but it wasn't easy. I was used to being able to ask Jessica if she liked something, and she always did. If I was freaked out about something, she was there to give a real opinion and tell me that it always turns out okay. At a certain point, I had to learn to ask myself whether things were going okay, whether it looked good or would turn out well. I did call her pretty much every damn day, and still do. However, I have, as has she, come to recognize that only we can really decide for ourselves if we are okay or going to be okay on any given day. We support each other in this, but the ultimate feel goods come from our own brains.

If you come from a close-knit, somewhat enmeshed family, not relying on praise, or even criticism, from others to get you through can feel confusing and awkward. You may also feel guilty that you have not included them in every single decision. That is all normal and totally okay. You and the people around you will benefit when you stop relying on others to see whether something passes muster and ask yourself first. Ultimately, you measure your opinion against everyone's else's.

Past versions of charm school or vintage glamour magazines advised you to look to your man or your mother to determine whether you passed muster. Now, we decide for ourselves whether we pass our definition of muster. We can appreciate and be grateful for the hype women we have in our lives. We can be thankful for what our mamas, grandmamas, and aunties have done for us and the foundation they have built by being bold, brave, and fierce. Ultimately, they will pass on, and it will be up to each woman to decide what type of gumption legacy she wants to leave behind and what new, brave, courageous, and determined way of showing up in the world she will model for the women coming behind her.

To begin, we must remember opinions are like a delicious buffet. The tables are laden high with food of all kinds. There is a hot vegetable section, carved meats, fruit, and an entire section dedicated to desserts. We want to jump to our favorite section and to get only the things we want. Then, something inside us tells us that we should look at the veggies and the fruit, and we do so begrudgingly. When the server offers us a plate of boiled broccoli, we find ourselves becoming angry and frustrated. We really want the damn dessert and the dinner rolls.

We suddenly forgot that we chose to go to the buffet. Nobody forced us to go. We also forgot that we decided to check out the vegetables and the fruit. It is not the server's fault that we rolled by that section, peered over, and even seemed interested. We were offered veggies, not force-fed vegetables and made to eat them with relish. In fact, we had the option to politely accept the vegetables and chuck them out later.

The same is true for our thoughts and the opinions that other people offer to us about our dreams and goals. Do not forget that we are the ones who opened our ears to their opinions, just like we wandered into the buffet. You may have even asked for someone's opinion, or it was offered to you. may have indicated that you want an opinion, just like you may have peered over that vegetable table. You are not required to act on an offered opinion. Like the boiled broccoli, you can graciously listen and accept the opinion, and chuck it later. Do not forget that anyone can offer you an opinion, but you can decide for yourself what you do with it.

You may decide you aren't going to do a damn thing about it. You listened, and that is where the action ends. Other people are entitled to their opinions and, my darling, so are you. What do you think? Do you think this was good enough? Did you like it? Did it meet your exacting standards? Did it pass muster with you? If not, I want to offer you a new way of approaching your work.

A- Work

I used to pride myself on "showing up excellent." This was a badge of honor to me, and everything I did was measured against this concept. It seemed in line with my love of the great generation during World War II and their spirit of excellence and can-do attitude. It sounds lofty enough, but it turned out to be quite insidious. My desire to be full of gumption and be excellent became a moving target, and a thinly-veiled cover for perfectionism. It was something that I would use against myself, and nothing was ever excellent or good enough. My quest to be a lady with gumption was exhausting, and I felt like I could never measure up to the imaginary perfect version of myself that was elegantly dressed and could, at a moment's notice, climb a mountain smiling.

I can now see how ludicrous it was to expect so much of myself. I can also see how I kept moving the target, so on day one, success meant one thing, and then on day two, the success marker had moved just out of my reach. It got to the point that I felt immobilized and defeated before I even began a project because I knew in my heart that it would never be good enough for me anyway. Then, I started to blame this way of thinking on other people around me.

My coach invited me to think about this in a new way. What if my work was not excellent, at least not all of the time, what would happen? Probably nothing. Would it be okay if I lowered my standard to B- work? That seemed heart-wrenching to me, so we settled on A.

What About A- Work?

A- work acknowledges that not everything will be done perfectly. You can't always expect perfection from yourself when usually B- or A- work really will do. It allows for small mistakes. When nitpicking begins making its way into your brain, you can remind your brain that A- work is accepted here. Of most import, it gets you working and creating again. It allows for a "done is better than perfect" attitude so you can actually create things AND show them to the world. An artist who paints the most beautiful painting but never stops tweaking it is unlikely to share that beautiful painting with the world. Don't keep what you have to offer the world under wraps because you believe it isn't perfect.

Imagine if scientists and inventors did not share what they were creating before it was perfected. We would probably still be waiting for the light bulb or automobile. Also, consider whether perfection is the lofty goal you think it is. Can you succinctly say when something has reached perfection? Knowing yourself as only you can, will today's definition of perfection put an end to tomorrow's critiques? In my experience, perfection is a moving target that allows you never to stop tweaking. It keeps us from sharing how far we've come with others. It keeps us from even beginning. It is insidious.

Perfection is for people who are too scared to be vulnerable in front of others and show progress. What if we started to value progress over perfection? What if we celebrate the piles of failures a success is built upon instead of the perceived success as an end game? An entrepreneur tells you their yearly revenue. Nice, but follow up those revenue numbers with, "How many lean years before that?" How many years spent in the red before that? How many years, my darling, before you started to break even? Usually, the businesses that are declared an overnight success are businesses whose failures were not touted in the same way as their successes. Those failures accumulated over seven years, so it looked like they were standing on a mountain of success, when actually it was a pile of failures.

The best way we can start to build a legacy of A- work that shows progress over perfection and celebrates the failures along the way is to begin modeling it ourselves. We need to celebrate our failures by accumulating more, evaluating, and trying again. A- work is the goal, allowing for your own small perceived mistakes. Send the product to your customers even if you don't perceive it as perfect. Your opinion about whether something is finished is paramount.

In short, the woman with gumption racks up failures, builds her success with A- work, and accumulates her failures in a pile until she is standing atop a vantage point that she declares to be a success. The story she tells about her failures and progress is her own New York sized story. She cultivates courage, determination, and initiative by deciding ahead of time that A- work will always be good enough and that all failures are welcome. After all, every good story has a good plot twist that includes failure and an eventual rise from the ashes.

Homework

For at least 10 minutes, free write all of your hopes, dreams, goals, and aspirations. (DO NOT CENSOR YOURSELF)

Look at that list and think about what you want to create over:

1. A lifetime
2. The next 10 years
3. The next 5 years
4. The next year
5. The next 3 months

What steps do you need to take to achieve your three-month goal? Include things you need to learn before you can take action steps, but don't let those things stop you from moving forward. Also, include anyone you need to speak to as part of your action plan

Think about how you will feel once you have achieved this three-month goal.

What thoughts will you need to practice to achieve that goal?

Think about every obstacle you will face, and write it all down.

Answer those obstacles with a strategy for overcoming that obstacle. If it is a negative thought, strategize how you will turn that negative thought into a neutral thought so you are not failing ahead of time.

When worry creeps in about all that you should have, could have, or would have done differently, write all of that ish down. Remember, it is a normal part of the process to have your brain nay-say you. Acknowledge it and keep it moving sis.

Of most import, think about the New York sized story you are writing. How will you tell this story to future generations? How will you tell this tale at a future dinner party? You are the leading lady of this story, so write yourself an epic part where you are the hero and get all of the best lines.

Podcast Episode Guide

Episode 11: The Should Committee

Episode 20: Comparison is a Biatch

Episode 33: Self Confidence

Episode 39: Perfectionism

Episode 42: Future Fabulous

Episode 61: Five Fabulous Questions

Bonus Episode: An Almost Life

PLUCK:
How to Show Up Like a Boss

Old vs. New

When I think of pluck, I think of an old-timey slang word that sounds cutesy. The actual meaning of the word is far from cutesy. It means fierce and determined courage in the face of difficulties. Pluck feels cutesy in modern times because the term has fallen out of regular use. I separate pluck from gumption because gumption is, in my mind, the action part, whereas pluck is the frame of mind needed to keep going. It is the courage part of the gumption equation and is deserving of special treatment.

Pluck is not just courage – it is determined courage. Remember, determination and courage are parts of the gumption trio. Put them together, and you have an entire way of being – you've got a pluck.

To have pluck does not mean we are robbed of charm, femininity, or softer skills. I think the woman with pluck is soft even in the face of adversity. She has not grown hard of heart and does not show up in the world jaded. Retaining her charm is part of her pluck.

In researching this chapter and reading stories of women's beauty regimens during World War II and times of rationing, I found two quotes that describe exactly what I am trying to convey to you, albeit better and more succinctly.

"To work for victory is not to say goodbye to charm. For good looks and good morale are the closest of allies." — 1940s Yardley advertisement.

Every charm and beauty book at that time promised if you mastered certain skills and behaviors, all would be right in the world, and you would achieve your wildest dreams. Those dreams, of course, were relegated to housekeeping and mothering for the most part, with the occasional rise to the secretary pool or becoming an actress.

Let's keep the notion that you can achieve your wildest dreams, but leave out the glass ceiling. You can do anything you want to do while also being feminine, charming, and fierce. You can work and keep the charm. This is not merely a matter of behavior modification, but a way of allying yourself with an exterior and interior congruent with one another. When the way you feel about yourself matches how you present yourself, and you work towards your own definition of victory while also maintaining that which makes you charming – that is pluck. You do not require yourself to be a workhorse, nor are you purely ornamental. Pluck allows both beauty and brains to operate at their highest. Life will bring you moments like those faced by women in the 1940s, who showed up to work, makeup and game face on. In 1942, *Vogue* declared, "Makeup is cherished, a last desperately defended luxury." Makeup was not trivial. Looking your best was not silly. Style was not trivial.

My grandmother died from complications related to lupus and diabetes. She was sixty-six years old, and by my standards, she was very young when she passed away. Even though she was sickly most of my childhood, there are a few key things about my grandmother that stick with me today. First was her smell. She always wore Carolina Herrera perfume, even when she was ill. To this day, my brain immediately picks out that scent in a crowd and I instinctively looks for and think about my grandmother. She smelled elegant, even when she was sick. She still wore cute house dresses and got prettied up. Eventually, she became wheelchair bound, but that did not stop her from showing up for life smelling and looking good. Those small acts of beauty were not trivial or silly. It was an important part of creating her own normality even if her body wasn't always cooperating. Her death found her smelling good and looking pretty. It found her in good spirits, still cracking jokes and laughing.

Whatever you may face in the future, how you dress and show up for the fray matters. Pluck helps you armor up in your mind and heart, with your makeup on. While the word may be old, the lessons it holds are always new. Life has a way of making lemons. We are here to make lemonade, serve it up in style, cultivate the seeds to make more lemons, and create an empire with a beautiful logo and branding from our lemonade stand.

In this final chapter, we will talk about looking at life with pluck.

Pluck As A Place

Gumption is the feelings that fuel our action, and pluck is a whole way of being. Consider that pluck is a location in your brain. I like to think of my prefrontal cortex living in the *Place of Pluck*. You are no longer in fight, flight, or freeze mode when you are in the place of pluck. You don't dwell on the past or over ruminate on a perceived mistake. It is a place of no regrets where you solve problems and your creative mojo is flowing.

Don't misunderstand. The place of pluck is not sunshine and rainbows, where everything comes easily and there are no problems. The opposite is true; you cannot get to the place of pluck unless you have failed many times and began again, in a new fashion. You cannot arrive at the place of pluck without experiencing hardship or adversity. The place of pluck is not for the faint of heart, but don't let that discourage you from attempting to cultivate a plucky attitude.

Know that in those moments when life feels most difficult and awful, you are nearing the place of pluck. You can circle on the road of despair or you can push ahead and get to the place where you can think with a forward-facing attitude. It takes a concerted effort to reach pluck. You must redirect your brain to that destination, much like you would a car. Your brain will want to take the highway and get there quicker, or not get in the car at all. Some days you may only drive by and get a glimpse and have to begin again tomorrow. That is perfectly okay. The idea is to get up every day, game face on, ready to drive, and get to the place of pluck.

Life is 50:50

There is a beautiful old Broadway Song, "Life is a bowl of cherries." Yes, indeed, it is, sweet juiciness with an unsuspecting hard-as-rock core that will break your teeth. Life is fifty percent negative and fifty percent positive. Without the pit, there would be no sweet cherry fruit. We cannot have one without the other. Having the expectation that life should be a technicolor dream gets us into the most trouble. The idea that things should be any other way than the way they are is a set up for assured disappointment.

I am not suggesting we give in to nihilism and surrender because death is inevitable. No, I think the opposite. When death arrives, will it find you doing what you set out to do, looking and smelling beautifully? It is entirely up to you. Just because you know death will come for you eventually does not mean that you should show up to life's party looking dowdy and frumpy.

The inevitability of my death or even the probability that I will experience hardship does not mean I should give up; instead, it is the very reason I choose to show up to my life in a very particular fashion. I have created my own set of rules and reminders for how I will show up to my life. Do I always nail it? No, but each day is a gift and an opportunity to try again.

My daily affirmation of who and whose I am is "I am beautiful. I am chic and stylish in dress. Elegant in manner and style. An encouragement. Feminine and Fierce. A blessing to those around me. I am enough. I am God's own daughter." I know that life is 50:50, and there are so many things outside of my control and purview, but for that which is within my purview, I take full responsibility.

"Life is like a bowl of cherries" is not a platitude but a recognition that life is both negative and positive. The expectation that I have to be happy and peppy all the time is BS and too much to expect of myself, or of anyone for that matter. It is also a farce that turned me into a people-pleasing maniac and left me exhausted and lonely. When I let go of that expectation, I could finally breathe and really be of service to others. Others around me could let go, too. We could all share the joy and the misery and make space for being human, both flawed and magnificent. I made room for both, and my life felt so much fuller.

It is important to differentiate yourself from a goal or unquestioned expectations that leave you feeling despair, defeat, and stuck. You continually ask yourself why you are failing to do something without ever formulating a concrete answer. Mostly because you have never stopped to examine if the expectation you have for yourself is something you even want to achieve. A goal that is truly yours will leave you feeling a bit barfy and exhilarated. The only way to know the difference is to check in with yourself and see if what you hope will happen differs from what you expect to happen.

How did I get to a place where I was able to drop expectations? First, I recognized that not everything would always be perfect and go according to plan. I embraced that life is 50:50 and I grew during times I perceived to be negative. I found that I needed those times as much as times where I felt more joy or peace. Neither the joy nor pain seemed to last very long. Second, I learned to ask myself better questions.

Asking Better Questions

The brain is wired for negativity, so when you ask it a leading question with negative bias built-in, it will automatically respond with craptastic answers. That's its job—to find the most negative answer. For example, when you wake up and ask your brain, "Why do I always feel like this?" it will tell you all sorts of horrible things to confirm why you feel terrible or dread that day. Ask your brain, "Why me?" and it will give you many negative examples to reinforce your beliefs about why bad things always happen to you. These types of questions have negativity built into them. They assume you already believe something crappy about yourself internally, no matter what occurs externally.

These kinds of questions leave no room for imagination or creative thinking because the inevitability of horrible things occurring is presumed in the question. It is hard to solve problems when you continually ask yourself, "Why does this keep happening?" It sounds like you are trying to solve a problem, but you have not asked your brain for a solution to move forward. You asked your brain to focus on the perceived mistake you continually make, ensuring that you are likely to repeat it.

It takes practice to recognize when you get into a negative question spiral. Most of us have catch phrases and questions we picked up as children that we repeat to ourselves without really noticing. When someone makes a statement like, "There is always something," it does not mean something good. It means something bad even when things are going well. How ominous and what an incredible joy stealer. I find myself saying things like this, too, and have to redirect my brain. It can be equally something good as bad, so the saying is unhelpful.

We must remind our brains that good things are as likely to occur as bad things because that's the nature of the 50:50 of life, no matter what your religious affiliation. The Bible states that "it rains on the just and the unjust" and "to everything there is a season." The seasons are both good and bad. Life is just doing its thing. We can always wait for something and lament our perceived situation with a "why me," or we can start to redirect our brains on purpose. We can show up with pluck and control that which is in our power to control. You have one of the most powerful tools in the world in your pluck arsenal, your brain. Now put it to work. "Woe is me" questions are not helpful and are mentally lazy. Do not let your brain run around unsupervised.

Five Fabulous Questions

Here are some recommended questions that will help set your brain running on the right track again. I call them the fab five questions because they are built for open-ended inquiry, positive affirmation, and problem-solving. Many of my clients ask themselves crappy questions, so they get crappy answers. Why am I so fat? Why am I so ugly? Why can't I ever seem to leave the house on time? Brains are wired to answer the questions we ask without filters. Our brains will tell us all the reasons we are fat, unworthy, and unstylish. If we do this long enough, we start to believe all of the crappy things our brains tell us. We get stuck in a negative thought loop, and it becomes our everyday reality.

Yup, that's right, boo-boo. Ask your brain crappy questions, and you will get crappy answers. How do I know our brains are wired to answer the questions we ask? Have you ever had someone ask you what song was playing? You remember the melody, but not the lyrics. Your brain goes crazy looking for the answer. A few hours pass, and you can still feel that low level hum of your mind working. After thinking for a few hours, ding ding ding your brain remembers! The song was… Suddenly, you feel a rush of relief.

Your brain is wired to answer the questions you ask it. Are you asking your brain the right questions? Are you asking yourself questions with unkind thoughts laced into them? Are the questions you're

asking skewed so they will only lead to net negative feelings and actions? Watch that Tallulah brain of yours. You can get unstuck. Get
out of that negative thought loop. Turn this whole negative thought
train around. How? By asking our brains better questions. Ask a better
question, and you'll get a better answer.

1. What would fabulous do?

This question is a great way to engage the plucky part of your brain
because there is a built-in positive assumption that you are the fabulous one doing the action. It presupposes your fabulousness and
ability to solve problems and engages the prefrontal cortex part of
your brain. This question is perfect for days when you feel stuck and
tell yourself there is no solution or way out. The regular tired worn-
out version of you may feel that way, but the plucky, fabulous version
of you knows what to do, or at the very least, how to get started. This
question becomes a great way to start your day. When you are getting
ready for the day, ask yourself, "What would fabulous do today?" It
will inform you how to get ready, what to wear, and how to choose to
take care of yourself throughout the day.

2. What would my future self wear/do?

This question is another one to engage the plucky part of your
brain. Perhaps you have issues believing that you are fabulous, so that
built-in presumption in the above question doesn't do it for you. Instead, remove the "fabulous" and insert "your future self." Your
future self has already solved the problem, made the decision, made
a choice, or has worked through the difficulty. When we engage our
imagination in this way and presuppose that we will have solved the
problem in the future, we have hope. Again, this question activates
the front part of your brain in charge of higher functioning and rea-
soning. It engages the plucky part of your brain that believes in
perseverance despite adversity.

I include the wear/do part here because when my clients get in a rut and always feel frumpy when getting ready, they cannot envision themselves moving past that feeling. Even after buying an entire new wardrobe, they still find themselves sitting on the edge of their bed in their undies down in the dumps. This question helps you look past the present moment of frumpy and look towards a day where perhaps you feel better. What would you choose on that day? Whatever your brain gives you to do or wear when it imagines that it's feeling better is a good place to start in the present moment, no matter how frumpy you may be currently feeling.

3. How do you really feel?

This question is perfect for those days when I find myself on a rant, and I'm talking *at* people instead of *to* them. I am over expounding and hyperbolically declaring the horrors of a present situation. I am all kinds of drama – fainting couch levels of ridiculous. Asking myself how I really feel allows me to snap myself back to reality without giving in to shame or self-condemnation. Like damn, OK, we get it, "Tell me how you really feel?" We all need space to rant and vent, but it does not need to be at people. This question is a snapback, but without the shame. Ask yourself this question, giggle at your level of dramatics, and then move it along sis, you have work to do. The question has built-in pluck and a bit of self-deprecation when you feel yourself being extra AF to your detriment.

4. What is the one thing I can do to make this so much better?

This is the perfect question to ask yourself when you have created something, spoken in public, or have finished a project but have a weird sensation of dissatisfaction. Something doesn't feel right about how it went. People congratulate you and tell you, "Well done," but you don't think it went as well as they were saying. The compliments fall flat. Rather than over ruminating on everything that could have gone wrong, stop and redirect your brain to the future focus. Access that place of pluck and ask what one thing you can do to make this better.

It presumes that it was already pretty good. After all, you can only make something "so much better" if it was already at some level of good. This presumes you succeeded at least at some level, but are looking to up your game. GO forth and conquer, but ask yourself useful questions about what you can do going forward rather than asking yourself, "What went wrong?" Remember, your brain will give you an answer, but it is likely not going to be as useful as asking yourself what is one (not ten million) thing you can do so much better?

5. What would I do/wear if I wasn't worried about what other people are thinking?

This is the perfect question for when the "should committee" starts going off in your head, and you find yourself hesitating or not taking action because you fear what other people will think. A variation on this thought is, "What would you do if you weren't afraid?" This allows you to be open-minded and engage the high-functioning part of your brain. When you ask yourself what people will think or what they will do if you take a certain action, your brain is likely to come up with answers that only confirm your own negative bias. Then, you are giving those thoughts more weight because you tell yourself that other people will think that, too.

This question is also really useful when you are confused about a decision that you need to make. You worry about making the right choice or the perfect decision. Usually, the need to make the right or ideal choice is driven by fear. You are afraid of making a mistake. If you weren't worried about what other people would think if you made a mistake, what would you do? Usually, the answer becomes clear when we allow your brain to imagine that it is neither afraid nor worried. The confusion ceases.

Why apply it to what you are going to wear? Because often, women are holding themselves back to style rules passed down from their grandmothers and mothers about what they should and should not wear. We would love to show up a certain way but are afraid of how other people will perceive us and fearful of what other people believe we think about ourselves. We cannot be too much, so we hold ourselves back not only in major life decisions but also in simple choices such as what we wear. When we eliminate others from the equation in our decision making, we can look more clearly at our fears and doubts instead of assigning that to others.

When my clients are in a spiral of worry about what other people think, I tell them to consider that your thoughts are just a series of electrical chemicals happening in your mind. A process that we call thought is occurring in your brain. Just like food passing through your colon is a process we call digestion. We spend almost no time considering what is going on inside other people's colons. We don't think about the acid turning food products to waste products. Why would we? That is creepy and weird. However, we spend an excessive amount of time focused on a process happening in people's brains: their thoughts. When we take it down to its base level, a process occurring in another person's body, we can hopefully be objective enough to see that we neither have control over that process, nor want to. This may sound silly, but sometimes it helps to reduce things to their base chemical process to objectively understand our lack of control and really our lack of desire to control. I have no desire to control the chemical process in other people's colons, so too, their brains. Really, at a base level, same difference.

Why the Fab Five Questions?

I have learned that some of us need a starting place. It is like trying to write a perfectly-crafted email, but you are at a loss for words. You ask a colleague for advice, but don't write down what they said, so by the time you get back to your office, you have completely forgotten their brilliant words. The Five Fabulous questions are a great jumping-off point. The answers to these questions give you words to start thinking about your everyday life differently. The idea is that you begin here and then craft your own set of five fabulous questions. Learn to craft your go-to glam squad of questions to get unstuck and be fabulous. The questions are not magical, but what your brain and imagination do with them is where the magic lies.

The beauty of the five fabulous questions is that they tap into the smarts you've already got. Yeah, you've got 'em. We must learn how to access those smarts. Look outside yourself for the answers. Yes, sometimes your brain will come up with a solution that requires you to ask for help or seek advice, that is smart. We often get in our own way and forget that we have solved problems or had breakthroughs in the past. We forget that other people are facing, or have faced, issues similar to ours and have persevered. Our brains get stuck in that loop because we expect to sit down and write a perfect email every time. That is impossible. Really think about that, do you always know exactly what to say every time? Nope, and don't make that mean anything in particular about you.

The same is true for most of life's decisions. We need a small jumping-off point, some words to get us going. A few lines to get that mojo word flowing. Use the five fabulous questions and take note when your brain expounds upon them, makes them better, and put them into your own words. Notice when you start to ask them in a variety of ways to those around you. Take notice of those moments when emails seem to flow or life seems to flow. It may not last, but it is a goldmine of information and a way to use those times for the 50:50 flipside of life that will inevitably come.

What's Pluck Got To Do With It?

Everything. It is that set of neurons in your brain firing with a can-do attitude that we need working. The future focused version of you looking forward to better and brighter days. The plucky part of you that shows up lovely to the everyday battles of life. A last look at a quote from the 1942-1943 Yardley beauty ads, "Let us face the future with heads held high. And let us always honor the subtle bond between good looks and good morale." This guide to modern charm is about being feminine and fierce but never hard. It is about engaging your beauty and your brains. This life is a short one, indeed, and generations after us will look to see how we showed up to the current difficulties with our game faces on.

We shall do our grandmothers, mothers, and our aunties proud by taking the very best they had to offer us by way of advice, practical glamour, and undermining misogyny in their own way during their time. We are now standing on the mountains of failures that they amassed, as well as their triumphs. In carving a path and modeling for the next generation behind us, we get to decide how we are going to show up, sit, stand, speak, dream, and do. In asking ourselves what our hopes, dreams, and aspirations are and then showing up to see that they are created, we are modeling pluck. It is one thing to admire pluck and stare at a picture of your grandmother from the 1940s and wistfully think about all she went through. It is another to reach out your hand and actively take from her all the best she had to offer to use in the world you currently live.

Confident women leave legacies, and I hope that after reading this book, you will take a closer and longer look at your beautiful forebears. Admire them. Really step into the black and white photo and think about the lessons you have learned. What do you want to take going forward? How do you want to level up your family legacy or write it entirely from scratch? What version of the big giant New York sized story will you tell? Better yet, what is the next chapter that you will write where you are the leading lady. Lovely, feminine, fierce, and ready to enter the fray full of pluck, gumption, and looking fly AF. If nothing else, my darling, commit to at least show up. In doing so, you are putting on the superhero cape, adding your own patch-work, and making it ready for the next woman. This is my love letter to you, my darling, and a thank you to my grandmother.

 **Homework**

Leading Lady Mission

Write a letter to yourself in the future one year from now. Give it to a trusted friend to hold onto or hide it away and set a timer on your phone to remind you to read the letter (and to remind you where you put the letter – I still haven't found one I wrote to myself in law school.)

1. Tell yourself about yourself. Write the story of your life thus far.
2. Write your biggest lessons.
3. Write your biggest worries.
4. Write your biggest hopes for the future.
5. List of current favorite items, clothing, perfume, makeup, treats, and books.

Write a letter to yourself from the future, and put this one away for a year. Act as though you have already solved your problems and have achieved what you have dreamed of achieving a year from now. You are where you want to be a year from now.

1. Give yourself advice on how you handled difficult situations.
2. Give yourself advice on how you handled relationships and difficult conversations.
3. Give yourself health and wellness advice.
4. List what you will have achieved and how you achieved it.
5. What were you feeling when you achieved that goal?

6. What were you thinking?

7. What did you let go of in order to get where you are?

8. How are you dressing? How are you feeling when you get ready? What are you thinking when you get ready in the morning?

9. What are your five fabulous questions?

Podcast Episode Guide

Episode 33: Self Confidence

Episode 39: Perfectionism

Episode 42: Future Fabulous

Episode 61: Five Fabulous Questions

Bonus Episode: An Almost Life

Conclusion:
Love Letter and a
Final Leading Lady Mission

My Darling,

Wherever you are right now, I want you to know that I am sending you all of my love. The fact that you and I are reading my words means that we have made it this far in life, which is no small feat. We are the product of a thousand mothers. You were a tiny egg inside of your mother, inside of your grandmother, who lived inside of your great grandmother, and so on. Your grandmother's story and life are interwoven with your own, for she helped carry you into this world. You are a living legacy of untold stories of women with pluck, gumption, and grit. After all, you have gotten this far.

Where you go from here is entirely up to you. Decide now to step into the role of a leading lady. Decide now to write a New York City sized dream. Decide now to show up face on, head high, and chin up. Model pluck and gumption for yourself and the other ladies watching you. Decide now to show up to your life in a way that makes the women watching you proud to take on the fabulous cape you leave behind for them.

Your Leading Lady Mission, should you choose to accept it, is to remember you are beautiful, confident, enough as you are, stylish and chic, elegant in manner, a force, and the leading lady. Now go forth with pluck and gumption.

Love,
Miss J

Made in the USA
Middletown, DE
07 July 2021